SpringerBriefs in Information Systems

Series editor

Jörg Becker

For further volumes:
http://www.springer.com/series/10189

Mathias Eggert

Compliance Management in Financial Industries

A Model-based Business Process and Reporting Perspective

 Springer

Mathias Eggert
Cologne
Germany

ISSN 2192-4929   ISSN 2192-4937   (electronic)
ISBN 978-3-319-03912-1   ISBN 978-3-319-03913-8   (eBook)
DOI 10.1007/978-3-319-03913-8
Springer Cham Heidelberg New York Dordrecht London

Library of Congress Control Number: 2013956630

Printed on acid-free paper

Springer is part of Springer Science+Business Media (www.springer.com)

Foreword

Since the world financial crisis, legislators all over the world have enacted new regulations and guidelines in order to monitor banks and to control their risk behavior. The compliance with regulatory requirements is often concerned with the compliant design of business processes and information systems. Due to the steady increase in regulations, this design effort challenges particularly the financial service industry. On the one hand, financial institutes must provide organizational structures to enable a proper collaboration of IT and legal experts when planning regulatory-compliant information systems. On the other hand, the frequency of enacted regulatory requirements increases steadily and forces financial institutes to react in a timely manner in order to prevent serious penalties or interruptions of business operations. The sum of all actions taken by an organization to respond appropriately to regulatory requirements are defined as compliance management—a research field that finds a growing interest, especially since the financial crisis.

Two types of regulatory requirements significantly affect financial institutions: requirements that primarily influence the business processes and requirements that primarily influence the supervisory reporting. Regulatory requirements on business processes are particularly relevant for the design of the organization, while supervisory requirements primarily affect the design of reporting and data warehouse systems. The growing number of regulations and more interconnected business processes lead to an increase of compliance management effort. The work of Mathias Eggert suggests model-based solutions for reducing this effort.

Motivated by the importance of information modeling for the successful design of information systems and business processes, Mathias Eggert investigates compliance management approaches from a business process and a data warehouse modeling perspective. He develops model-based approaches to analyze the effects of legal requirements on business processes and data warehouses. In addition, he gives insights into the influence of regulation on the design of information systems and suggests solutions for the improvement of the collaboration between IT and legal experts. The promising results are a valuable contribution to the improvement of information systems in the financial service industry.

Münster, July 16, 2013   Jörg Becker

Acknowledgments

"Falling is neither dangerous nor a disgrace. Staying down is both."

Konrad Adenauer

The story that ends up in this book is not as usual, as it is for other researchers. In the beginning of my life, I did not think about a scientific career. At the age of 18, when others think about their study topic and university to visit, the scientific path was even not in my mind. Rather, I was convinced that a more practical oriented way would characterize my career. After graduation at the junior high school, a scientific career was so far away that nobody, including myself, would have thought that I would ever write a dissertational thesis. My career began with an apprenticeship at a logistic company close to my hometown Cologne. After a couple of years of working for different companies, I realized that I had to change my life completely in order to get new challenges. Thus, I decided to leave the practical level in order to go back into learning and to visit high school for getting the permission to study. At the age of 24, I finally began studying Information Systems in the city of Ingolstadt.

"Et hätt noch emmer joot jejange," a traditional proverb from the German city of Cologne, says that each change in life will finally end up successfully. Writing this book was the end of a story that is about many people who trusted me, who motivated me, and who never gave up telling me that also my winding way will end up successfully. Without their help and support, these lines would not exist. The following pages are for all of these wonderful people.

Studying is expensive, even in Germany, where usually no study fees have to be paid. The study costs usually forces students to work besides their lectures and learning sessions. During my study, I could completely focus on my study because I received two scholarships during the Bachelor and Master phases. Therefore, I thank the Siemens AG for their financial support and the chance to attend in several workshops and seminars. I especially thank the Konrad Adenauer Foundation, which strongly supported my Master's program and the research project that led to the results published in this book. I do not know whether I would be able to write these lines without the support of these great organizations.

Successful research that aims to produce valuable results for the industry always needs good industry partners, which trust in the ability to create innovative ideas and successful results. During the past 4 years I especially built-up strong ties with an IT service provider in Muenster, whose employees always supported my ideas. Therefore, I especially thank Thorsten Webering and Daniel Vohrmann for their great support of this research project. Without their continuous availability for workshops and interviews, I could not reflect industry expectations for compliance management systems. Furthermore, I thank all the students who worked in the numerous project seminars I supervised. In particular, the collaboration with Sebastian Schwittay and Friedrich Chasin supported my research work.

I will always remember the time as researcher at the IS department of the University of Muenster. In particular, the "researcher beer," the numerous conference trips, and the fun I had during the holidays afterwards. I especially thank Matthias Voigt for the great trips to Moscow and Marcel Heddier for the great collaboration and time in Australia. I also thank my supervisors Jörg Becker, Ralf Knackstedt, and Patrick Delfmann. They have taught me how to research and how to publish scientific papers. Without their critical reflection and openness for new ideas, this doctoral thesis would not exist in the way it does.

However, all fruitful ideas and scientific discourses need two essential resources: family and friends. My friends were there for me, when I was disappointed about a bad grade or rejected papers. They always motivated me to go on studying and finally they strengthened my wish to begin the Ph.D. program. Particularly, I thank my close friends Dirk, Hans Peter, Jan, Regina, Stephie, and Susanne for their great support at all times since I decided to follow the scientific path.

Finally, I would like to express my deepest gratefulness to my parents, Günther and Irma, as well as my sister Claudia. They always supported my way of life and gave me love. At any time, I could count on their help—in particular in hard times, when life was not shiny and successful. I dedicate this work to my family.

Cologne, October 13, 2013   Mathias Eggert

Contents

Abbreviations

ACIS	Australasian Conference on Information Systems
ADAPT	Application Design for Processing Technologies
BPCL	Business Process Compliance Language
BPEL	Business Process Execution Language
BPM	Business Process Management
BPMN	Business Process Modeling Notation
BPR	Business Process Reengineering
BPSL	Business Property Specification Language
CIO	Chief Information Officer
CNF	Conference Paper
CRD	Capital Requirements Directive
DFM	Dimensional Fact Model
DSRM	Design Science Research Methodology
DW	Data Warehouse
ECIS	European Conference on Information Systems
ERM	Entity Relationship Model
ETL	Extracting, Transforming, and Loading
EU	European Union
FCL	Formal Contract Language
FSM	Finite State Machine
H2fR	H2 for Reporting
HICSS	Hawaii International Conference on System Sciences
IFRS	International Financial Reporting Standard
IS	Information Systems
IT	Information Technology
ITSP	IT Service Provider
JNL	Journal Paper
JQ2.1	Jourqual 2.1
LTL	Linear Temporal Logic
MaRisk	Minimum Requirements for Risk Management
ME	Method Engineering
ME/RM	Multidimensional Entity Relationship Modeling
MiFID	Markets in Financial Instruments Directive
MIS	Management Information Systems
MISQ	Management Information Systems Quarterly
MKWI	Multikonferenz Wirtschaftsinformatik
OLAP	Online Analytical Processing
OLTP	Online Transaction Processing
PBB	Process Building Block

PCL	Process Compliance Language
PCML	Process Constraint Modeling Language
PLS	Partial Least Squares
PPML	Process Pattern Modeling Language
RQ	Research Question
SBPML	Semantic Business Process Modeling Language
SEC	Securities and Exchange Commission
SEM	Structural Equation Modeling
SimBPEL	Simplified syntax Business Process Execution Language
SOX	Sarbanes Oxley Act
TAM	Technology Acceptance Model
UML	Unified Modeling Language
US-GAAP	United States Generally Accepted Accounting Principles
WI	Wirtschaftsinformatik
WKWI	Wissenschaftliche Kommission Wirtschaftsinformatik
WpDVerOV	Wertpapierdienstleistungs-, Verhaltens- und Organisationsverordnung
WpHG	Wertpapierhandelsgesetz
WS-BPEL	Web Service Business Process Execution Language
XBRL	eXtendable Business Reporting Language
XML	eXtendable Markup Language

Chapter 1
Introduction

1.1 Motivation

Since the U.S. American bank Lehman Brothers ran into bankruptcy on September 15th 2008, global economy was pushed into a heavy recession. Two main reasons for this financial crisis were broadly discussed: an extremely unregulated stock and securities trading market as well as very leisurely equity regulations (Acharya and Richardson 2009; Crotty 2009). According to Goodhart (2008) the regulatory response to the crisis primarily affected at least seven major fields in financial regulation: (1) The form of deposit insurance, (2) the bank solvency regimes, (3) the money operations of central banks, (4) the liquidity risk management requirements of commercial banks, (5) the capital adequacy ratio requirements (Basel III was introduced), (6) the boundaries of regulation (conduits and structured investment vehicles are stronger regulated), (7) as well as domestic and cross-border crisis management (Goodhart 2008). This body of regulation is "normally extended incrementally, frequently to close a loophole which some earlier fraud or financial disaster has exposed" (Brunnermeier et al. 2009, p. 1). Meanwhile, the financial sector is perceived as "the most heavily regulated industry" (Abdullah et al. 2010, p. 254).

The accelerated growth of the regulatory body has serious consequences for financial institutes in general and for their management of regulatory compliance in particular. The effort to manage the steady change of regulations and its impact on the organization is increasingly challenging (Abdullah et al. 2010). An industry study stating that the spending for ensuring compliance exceeds 32B US$ in 2008 (McGreevy 2008) confirms this challenge. Furthermore, compliance is regarded as one of the most important information security issues, and was considered to be even more important than malicious software (Ernst and Young 2005).

Regulations impact financial institutions primarily in two ways. They influence the design and execution of the respective business processes and they influence financial reporting, in particular supervisory reporting. Currently the German Federal Reserve provides forms for 136 different reports that supervised banks are required to submit frequently to different authorities (Bundesbank 2012). From a

M. Eggert, *Compliance Management in Financial Industries*,
SpringerBriefs in Information Systems, DOI: 10.1007/978-3-319-03913-8_1,
© The Author(s) 2014

business process perspective, business processes of the financial industry are affected, for instance, by the German Banking Law, the Minimum Requirements for Risk Management (MaRisk) (BaFin 2011), and several guidelines, such as the Investment Services Conduct of Business and Organization Regulation.

In today's banks, both business processes and financial (supervisory) reporting are heavily supported by specific Information Systems (IS) (Bonsón et al. 2010; Pfeiffer and Flöck 2011). IS play a significant role in the industrialization and improvement of a bank's process efficiency. The trend towards a continuous business process reengineering (BPR) further increased the importance of IS (Davenport and Beers 1995; Davenport and Stoddard 1994; Hammer and Champy 1993). Along with rethinking and redesign of business processes, business process managers are confronted with a vast amount of (regulatory) compliance requirements. Not all measures that promise to increase process efficiency comply with regulations. Thus, banks need to check whether a business process change request complies with all relevant regulations.

The implementation of compliant business processes as well as the development of regulatory compliant IS require that all stakeholders, such as Information Technology (IT) and legal experts, collaborate closely in the requirements engineering phase of an IS project. Therefore, conceptual modeling techniques support the formal description of aspects of the physical and social world. They aim at improving the understanding and communication among stakeholders (Mylopoulos 1992). The development process of an IS comprises the usage of conceptual models because they allow for an early detection and correction of IS design mistakes (Wand and Weber 2002). While the development of business requirements for IS was investigated in many studies and is well-known (e.g., Gordijn and Akkermans 2003; Karlsson et al. 2002; Weber and Weisbrod 2002), regulatory requirements for IS design differ from such business requirements fundamentally and need further attention. "Specifying legally compliant requirements is challenging because legal texts are complex and ambiguous by nature" (Massey et al. 2012, p. 1). The complexity and vast amount of regulatory requirements ask for new ways of collaboration between the stakeholders of regulatory-driven IT projects. In fact, this raises the question whether the traditional requirements engineering methods and tools are still feasible for IT projects in a regulatory environment.

The challenge to design and check conceptual regulatory compliant IS requirements specifications strongly demands for software solutions that support financial institutes in managing the impact of regulatory requirements. However, current approaches for managing compliance challenges and regulatory impacts do not fulfill all practitioners' needs (Abdullah et al. 2010). Rather than developing solutions, which assist organizations in managing regulatory requirements, IS research currently focuses on exploratory studies (Abdullah et al. 2009). The book at hand addresses this research gap and sheds light on methods and guidelines to support the compliant design of reporting systems and business processes in financial industries.

1.2   Research Questions

In order to support compliance management in financial industries, this book follows four research questions. First, the impact of regulations on IS development processes is investigated and possible research artifacts that cope with the conceptualization of model-based compliance management need to be classified. Therefore, the first research question is:

To what extent do regulations influence the conceptual specification of information systems (RQ1)?

From an organizational perspective, RQ1 is addressed by investigating the influence of regulation on the organization and the management of IT departments and IT service providers (RQ1.1). From a technical perspective, IS research artifacts that support model-based compliance management are classified (RQ1.2).

The second research question addresses the need to develop and evaluate an approach for improving the efficiency and effectiveness of business process compliance management:

How can the efficiency and effectiveness of business process compliance checking be improved (RQ2)?

This question is answered by shedding light on five aspects. From a design science perspective, the problem needs to be identified and the research work needs to be motivated (Peffers et al. 2007). Therefore, a brief literature review should provide insights into the state of the art of business process compliance checking approaches (RQ2.1a). Based on these insights, a roadmap for further research in this field is developed (RQ2.1b). In order to provide a solution that addresses RQ2.1, a compliance management approach is developed that allows for checking business process models for the fulfillment of compliance requirements (RQ2.2). From a behavioral science perspective RQ2 is addressed in two ways. First, an evaluation concept for proving the relevance and applicability of business process compliance checking approaches is developed for financial industry case studies (RQ2.3). Second, the concept is applied empirically in a financial industry case in order to get insights into the applicability and relevance of the developed artifact (RQ2.4).

Besides the fulfillment of business process compliance requirements, banks must also comply with regulatory reporting requirements (Bundesbank 2012). Therefore, the third research question addresses model-based compliance management for supervisory reporting:

How can the efficiency and effectiveness of the conceptual specification of regulatory reporting requirements be improved (RQ3)?

This research question is answered with respect to four aspects. The challenges of designing requirement specifications in a regulatory environment are identified and discussed (RQ3.1). Based on the problem identification, a suitable modeling technique is developed and evaluated in terms of efficiency and effectiveness (RQ3.2). The aspect of applicability of the developed modeling technique is addressed by an implementation of a modeling tool that allows regulatory analyses of conceptual models (RQ3.3). Finally, the modeling technique's capabilities to represent regulatory reporting requirements are investigated (RQ3.4).

Anytime when IS needs to be redesigned, for example, in order to comply with a changed regulatory environment, a common ground (Clark and Brennan 1996) with respect to system requirements needs to be established (Bashar and Easterbrook 2000; Mylopoulos 1998). Therefore, the last research question copes with the collaboration of IS experts and legal experts in regulatory-driven IT and research projects:

How can the collaboration of IT experts and legal experts be characterized and supported in research and practice (RQ4)?

The collaboration of IT experts and legal experts is investigated from a practical perspective (RQ4.1) as well as from a research perspective (RQ4.2). While from a practical perspective IT experts from the industry are the main subject of investigation, the investigated subjects of the research perspective are IS researchers and their perception of the relationship between IS and law. Finally, RQ4 is addressed by the development of a research portal in order to classify and analyze the interdisciplinary research artifacts from information law and legal informatics (RQ4.3).

1.3 Book Structure

This book presents the essence of several research articles published in different scientific journals and conferences. These articles served as a foundation for my cumulative doctoral thesis. Besides the topic motivation and a brief introduction into compliance management in financial industries, the work briefly describes the relationship of the research results. The remainder is structured as follows: Chap. 2 provides an overview of the research background, which comprises the state-of-the-art in business process modeling and compliance analysis, data warehouse development, multisensory law, legal visualization, and foundations of regulatory requirements engineering. In Chap. 3 the applied research paradigm and research methods are described. Chapter 4 provides a synopsis of the research results and describes its contribution to answer the research questions (RQ1–RQ4). Chapter 5 discusses the research findings and gives a research outlook. The book structure is depicted in Fig. 1.1. Each grey shaded area comprises a section in the book and each black area comprises one research outcome.

The first set of publications (Becker et al. 2012c; Eggert et al. 2013b) identifies the relevance of and provides findings about model-based compliance management (RQ1). The second set of publications provides research results regarding the improvement of business process compliance checking (RQ2). The corresponding findings are published in three publications (Becker et al. 2011a, 2012a, e). The third set of publications (Becker et al. 2012b, d; Eggert et al. 2013a) contains findings regarding the improvement of conceptual modeling and the analysis of

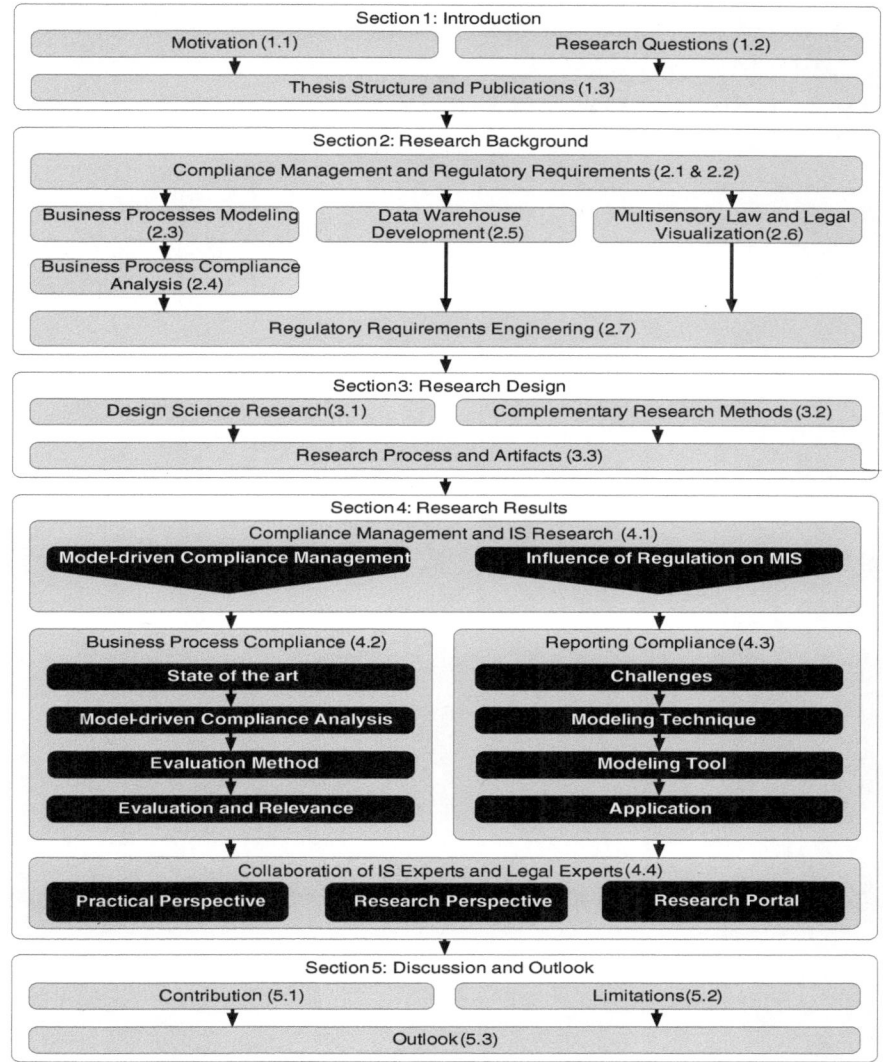

Fig. 1.1 Book structure

regulatory reporting requirements (RQ3). Chapter 4 addresses the collaboration of IS experts and legal experts (RQ4). Corresponding research results are provided in three publications (Knackstedt et al. 2010, 2012, 2013).

Chapter 2
Research Background

2.1 Compliance Management and Regulatory Requirements

The body of regulation for financial service providers increases steadily and even faster after the world financial crisis of 2008. Corresponding regulation initiatives aim at closing gaps which the financial crisis has exposed (Brunnermeier et al. 2009). Two major streams of compliance requirements for financial institutes exist. One stream focuses on the proper design and execution of business processes (business process compliance), while the other stream focuses on bank supervision and financial reporting requirements. Both types of regulatory requirements need to be addressed by compliance management activities.

The literature provides different definitions of the term compliance management. Abdullah et al. (2009) define compliance management as "mechanisms to keep enterprise's businesses safe from possible violation of regulatory compliance" (Abdullah et al. 2009, p. 2). A broader definition is provided by El Kharbili et al. (2008b), who perceive compliance management as "the term referring to the definition of means to avoid [...] illegal actions by controlling an enterprise's activities. By extension, compliance management also refers to standards, frameworks, and software used to ensure the company's observance of legal texts" (El Kharbili et al. 2008b, p. 2). According to Karagiannis (2008), compliance management comprises three elements: the regulatory approach to ensuring the conformance with regulations and corporate governance, the standardization approach, which ensures conformance with standards, such as provided by ISO, and the corporate standards/best practices approach, which ensures the conformance with best practice frameworks. In this book, the term compliance management is defined as the sum of all organizational and technical activities that support the alignment of business processes and information systems with regulatory requirements.

According to an industry study among compliance experts, Abdullah et al. (2010) identifies seven major compliance management challenges, of which italic marked challenges are particularly addressed in this book:

M. Eggert, *Compliance Management in Financial Industries*,
SpringerBriefs in Information Systems, DOI: 10.1007/978-3-319-03913-8_2,
© The Author(s) 2014

- Lack of Compliance Culture
- *High Cost*
- Lack of Efficient Risk Management
- Difficulties in Creating Evidence of Compliance
- Lack of Perception of Compliance as Value-add
- *Lack of Understanding of its Relevance to Business*
- *Lack of Communication among Staff*

The lack of compliance culture comprises all cultural impacts of compliance on the organization. Many organizations do not support compliance issues properly; for instance, they do not provide management support or assign junior or "non-star" resources to compliance issues only. The cost issue of fulfilling compliance requirements hinders organizations to implement compliance frameworks. Small and medium sized companies are particularly affected by compliance costs because they do not have the capacity to manage compliance issues. The lack of efficient risk management addresses the resistance to allocate sufficient resources to identify and manage enterprise risks. Difficulties in creating evidence of compliance refer to the organization's inability to demonstrate and prove that the organization is compliant. This challenge especially requires the controlling and recording of compliance-relevant incidents. The identified lack of perception of compliance as a value-add summarizes challenges of establishing a common sense about the value of compliance. Many companies do not perceive compliance as a benefit. Rather, they feel that compliance complicates businesses and that it provides no benefit for the business. This provokes the lack of understanding of compliance relevance to business. Organizations must ensure that relevant regulations for their business are identified and that employees understand these requirements. Finally, the lack of communication among staff refers to the challenge of establishing efficient communication channels within the organization. This lack addresses the problem of communicating regulatory changes and their impact on organizations' activities (Abdullah et al. 2010). This book addresses in particular three challenges:

- *High costs* are addressed by the developed business process compliance checking and report modeling approaches, which support compliance checking tasks.
- *The lack of understanding of compliance relevance to business* and the *difficulties in creating evidence of compliance* are supported by the analysis capability of the approaches developed, which enables searching for regulatory affected business processes and reports. In addition, compliance frauds can be detected.
- The developed modeling technique for regulatory reporting requirements aims at building a common ground between system engineers and legal experts, which addresses the *lack of communication among staff*. The communication aspect will also be addressed by investigating the collaboration of IS and legal experts.

2.2 Regulatory Environment of Banks

Financial institutions are, in comparison to other industry sectors, heavily regulated. Barth et al. (2004) provides five main reasons for restricting bank activities. First, conflicts of interests appear when banks act in business areas, such as securities underwriting or real estate investment, and ill-informed investors need to be advised. Second, "moral hazard encourages riskier behavior" (Barth et al. 2004, p. 209). If a more risk taking behavior is allowed, banks will increase their investment risks to engage in more market activities. Third, the more complex a bank is, the more complex it is to monitor such a bank. Fourth, such large banks may become political and economically powerful that they are too big to fail. Fifth, large financial institutes prevent market competition and reduce market efficiency (Barth et al. 2004). In order to address these five reasons, mainly two regulatory types of requirements exist which are described next: regulatory business process requirements and supervisory reporting requirements.

2.2.1 Regulatory Business Process Requirements

Business processes in financial institutes are regulated through many different laws. They mainly come from three different sources: Legislation and regulatory bodies, for instance, Sarbanes–Oxley Act (*SOX*), Markets in Financial Instruments Directive (MiFID) and Basel III, standards and practical guidelines (e.g., SCOR, ISO9000), as well as business partner contracts (Governatori and Rotolo 2010). Relevant process compliance requirements for banks can be found, for example, in the MaRisk (BaFin 2011), the Securities Trading Act (ger. Wertpapierhandelsgesetz (WpHG)) and the Investment Services Conduct of Business and Organization Regulation (ger. Wertpapierdienstleistungs, Verhaltens- und Organisationsverordnung (WpDVerOV)).

One prominent example for a business process compliance requirement in financial industries is the obligation to handout consulting protocols (§14 WpHG, §14, Section 6 WpDVerOV). According to Section 5 of the Investment Services Conduct of Business and Organization Regulation, a customer must receive adequate information about the financial products offered in a financial consultation process. In addition, according to Section 14, the financial service provider must prepare a consultation protocol and is obligated to hand it over to the customer. Figure 2.1 graphically depicts a process excerpt with the corresponding protocol handout requirement. The bold framed elements comprise the process elements that are necessary for fulfilling the handout requirement. Such a set of process elements may be a part of a structural pattern, which can be applied for detecting compliance frauds in several business process models.

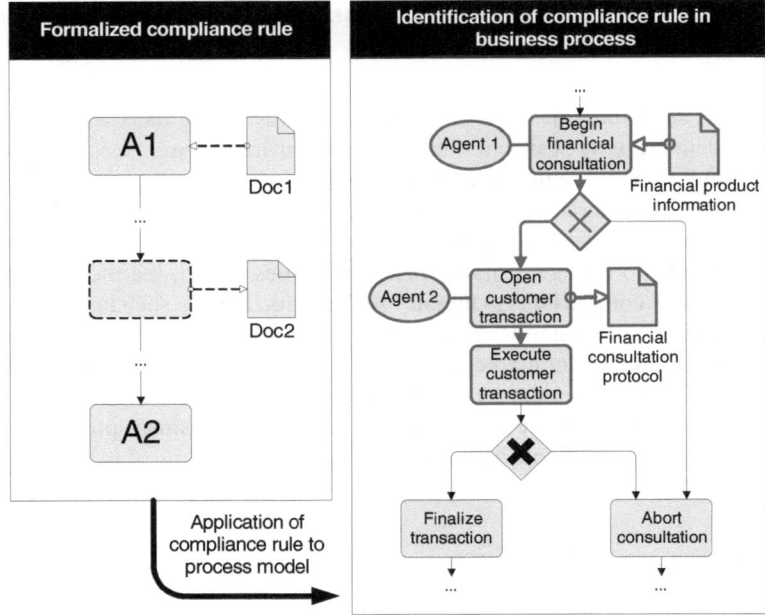

Fig. 2.1 Exemplary business process compliance requirement. Adapted from Becker et al. (2012a)

2.2.2 Supervisory Reporting Requirements

To monitor banks, supervisory agencies require information regarding the full range of activities and risk management procedures (BaFin 2011). In addition, the reporting of adequate capital according to regulations, such as Basel or its transformation into European law through the EU Capital Requirements Directive (CRD) (Bongaerts and Charlier 2009), as well as the reporting of credit information (in particular large exposures) to a central institution is of evident importance (Barron and Staten 2003; Cowan and de Gregorio 2003; Tsai et al. 2011). Besides these banking specific disclosure requirements, several general reporting regulations, such as the International Financial Reporting Standard (IFRS) or the United States Generally Accepted Accounting Principles (US-GAAP), need to be followed. According to Craig and Diga (1996) reporting regulations can be classified in three different dimensions:

Table 2.1 Excerpt of reporting requirements according to the MiFID regulation

Required information to fulfill reporting requirements for the execution of customer orders	Required information to fulfill reporting requirements in financial portfolio management
(a) The name of the company that creates the message	(a) Name of the investment service company (WpDLU)
(b) The name or other designation of the customer	(b) The name and designation of the account
(c) The trading day	(c) The composition and evaluation of the portfolio with details of any financial instrument
(d) The trading time	
(e) Type of order	(d) Total accrued charges and fees, which are splitted by at least total management fees and total costs, and a note that a detailed description is sent on request
(f) The place of execution	
(g) Financial instrument	
(h) Purchase/selling indicator	
(i) The nature of the order if it is not a purchase or sell order	(e) Comparison of performance with a benchmark
(j) Quantity	(f) Total amount of dividends, interest and other payments during the reporting period
(k) Unit price	
(l) Total price	(g) Information on other measures of WpDLU, rights regarding owned financial instruments, lend financial instruments and for each executed transaction within the reporting period the Information from (c) to (i) from the left column, in case the customer does not require a separate listing for each transaction
(m) Invoiced commission	
(n) Customer tasks related to the order execution	
(o) A note, if the contracting party of the investment service company (WpDLU) was the company itself or a person or group to which the WpDLU is a member of, or if it was a customer of the WpDLU	

Adapted from Becker et al. (2007a)

- Financial reporting-related legislation, which contains all reporting regulations that can be found in companies' laws, securities laws and tax statutes.
- Official directives and guidelines issued by government agencies, which comprise regulations, such as companies' law administrators, securities market regulators and tax authorities.
- Rules and guidelines, issued by private sector organizations, comprise all regulations that are posted by professional accountancy bodies and stock exchanges.

Regulations such as IFRS and US-GAAP, for example, can be assigned to the category of financial reporting-related legislation. In this book, all three dimensions of regulations are considered, since all regulatory requirements are investigated regarding their relevance for IS design. In the following, the term regulation is used for laws, directives, acts, rules, recommendations, and other principles, which are relevant for financial report design.

The financial industry in Germany has several different supervisory reporting requirements. On its web page the German Federal Bank summarizes all regulatory-driven reports that have to be generated by German banks. Depending on the business environment of a bank, up to 136 reports need to be generated (Bundesbank 2012). In order to exemplarily demonstrate the content of such a report, Becker et al. (2007a) summarizes a part of the report requirements for the MiFID, which was implemented into German law in 2007. Parts of such reporting obligations, which can be seen as data requirements for a data warehouse, are summarized in Table 2.1.

Disclosure regulations and their electronic transformation are strongly related to each other. Nowadays, the electronic exchange of regulatory required reports is prominently supported by using the data exchange standard XBRL (eXtendable Business Reporting Language). XBRL is based on the eXtendable Markup Language (XML) and enables the automated production and consumption of financial reporting and performance information (Bergeron 2004). Corporate information can be incorporated directly into the data warehouse systems of information consumers, such as the Securities and Exchange Commission (SEC) or other stakeholders (Debreceny et al. 2010). Since its initial usage within the Australian Prudential Regulatory Authority in 2002, XBRL has been adopted within several other regulatory directives and guidelines (Kernan 2008; Williams et al. 2006). Authorities like the SEC or European supervisory authorities describe financial reporting obligations by using the data exchange standard XBRL (Bergeron 2004; Debreceny and Gray 2001). Moreover, XBRL becomes the central data exchange standard in the area of credit monitoring and reporting corporate performance (Debreceny 2007). With its standardization potential, XBRL makes an important contribution to a non-ambiguous and well-defined data transfer between firms and supervisory authorities.

2.3 Business Process Modeling

Business processes are the central point of process-oriented corporate design. While an organizational structure divides an organization into task-oriented units, such as divisions and departments, business processes deal with the execution of these tasks (Becker and Kahn 2003). Davenport defines a process as "structured sets of work activity that lead to specified business outcomes for customers" (Davenport and Beers 1995, p. 57). A business process is directed by business objects and is influenced by a company's environment (Becker and Kahn 2003).

Nowadays, companies try to conceptualize their business processes in order to reduce complexity, increase understanding, and uncover optimization potential. Therefore, conceptual business process modeling techniques are applied (Aguilar-Savén 2004; Bandara et al. 2005; Rosemann 2003). "Conceptual modelling is the activity of formally describing some aspects of the physical and social world around us for purposes of understanding and communication" (Mylopoulos 1992, p. 50). Conceptual models play a significant role in IS development as they allow for an early detection and correction of IS design mistakes (Wand and Weber 2002). Business process models have received even more attention since the business process reengineering trend in the early 1990s came up (Davenport and Stoddard 1994; Hammer and Champy 1993). Several business process modeling techniques have been developed. According to an industry study of Becker et al. (2010a), the most relevant modeling techniques in financial industries are the Business Process Modeling Notation (BPMN) (Object Management Group 2006), Event-driven Process Chains (EPC) (Keller et al. 1992), and the activity diagrams from the Unified Modeling Language (UML) (Object Management Group 2005).

All these modeling techniques have in common that they are not domain-specific and that they can be applied for several purposes. According to Pfeiffer (2008), these properties come along with a couple of deficiencies: semantic inequality conflicts, such as homonym conflicts, semantic equality conflicts, such as synonym conflicts, and order conflicts. These identified problems of classical modeling techniques lead to the development of building block-based modeling techniques, which are semantically enriched by a domain ontology and standardized through the usage of predefined building blocks. Process building blocks are reoccurring activities in a certain business domain (Baacke et al. 2010; Becker et al. 2007b; Lang and Bodendorf 1997; Pfeiffer 2008). One example for a building block-based modeling technique is the PICTURE notation, which was developed for modeling business processes in the public administration (Becker et al. 2007b). Adapting the idea of building blocks for the financial industry, a domain-specific process modeling technique for banks has been developed (Becker et al. 2010b; Weiß 2011).

2.4 Business Process Compliance Analysis

Several compliance-checking approaches have been developed in order to ensure that business processes follow regulatory requirements. The major goal of this research stream is either to ensure that a business process fulfills all regulatory and business requirements or to detect compliance frauds after the execution of a business process. El Kharbili et al. (2008a) separates approaches for the analysis of business process compliance in two time-dependent classes: forward compliance checking and backward compliance checking. Forward compliance checking approaches aim to detect compliance frauds and analyze business processes with respect to the fulfillment of compliance rules before (design-time compliance) or while they are executed (run-time compliance). Hence, the processes are checked during the design-time or execution- time. Backward compliance checking approaches check whether a compliance fraud has appeared in the past. Thus, backward compliance checking approaches allow for a retrospective analysis of concrete process instances (El Kharbili et al. 2008a). This book solely focuses on design-time compliance. In the remainder of this section, the requirements for compliance checking approaches and common forward, run-time, and backward compliance checking approaches are discussed.

2.4.1 Requirements for Compliance Checking Approaches

The business process compliance checking approach, developed in this book, is guided by the fundamental requirements for supporting semantic constraints, such as business rules or policies, in process management systems (Ly et al. 2012):

- Formal language for constraint specification: A modeling language for expressing compliance requirements and process constraints that allows for a formal analysis is required.
- Constraint organization: A way to organize semantic constraints, such as compliance rules, is necessary. The use of repositories (Ly et al. 2006) or directories for such constraints (Sadiq et al. 2007) is suggested (Ly et al. 2012).
- Views on semantic constraints at different abstraction levels: Compliance rules must be represented differently with respect to their viewer, i.e., business and legal experts need a different view on compliance rules than tool and implementation experts.
- Support of lifetime compliance: The compliance of business processes must be analyzable during design-time and run-time. In addition, a process management system must allow for validating process instance changes and process model adaptations.
- Support process-spanning scenarios: The compliance management system must allow for validating multiple processes and process instances at once.
- Providing intelligible feedback: The user of a compliance management system should get comprehensive feedback, i.e., providing an error diagnosis, advices for conflict resolutions, and compensation strategies.
- Support of flexible constraint handling: The approach must allow for classifying compliance requirements according to enforcement levels and enforcement strategies, such as "only a bank branch manager may skip the personal customer identification". Hence, it must be possible to establish a relation between organizational units and compliance rules.
- Support of traceability: The results of each compliance check must be documented properly in order to enable the reconstruction of the past compliance checks and its results. In particular, compliance audits require this feature.

2.4.2 Design-Time Compliance Checking

Design-time compliance checking approaches belong to the group of forward compliance checking approaches and work on process models that are not yet deployed and thus can be changed without consequences for running process instances. The approach of Foerster et al. (2007) allows for checking quality constraints on business processes automatically. The authors specify simple control-flow patterns and formalize them using Linear Temporal Logic (LTL) (for LTL see Clarke et al. 2000). In order to execute a pattern search, the approach makes use of the NuSMV model checker (Cimatti et al. 2002). The result is binary, expressing whether the process model is compliant or not.

Another research stream focuses on the development of modeling techniques for compliance rules as one element for the model checking approach. In many cases these approaches use or extend the Formal Contract Language (FCL) (Governatori and Milosevic 2006; Governatori et al. 2006; Governatori and Rotolo 2010). The approaches detect missing or prohibited activities within a process model. The Process Compliance Language (PCL), which extends FCL, combines defeasible logic and deontic logic and allows for formalizing exceptions, violations and obligations (Governatori and Rotolo 2010). Based on these findings, Lu et al. (2008a; 2008b) developed an algorithm that enables the quantification of the effort that is needed to transform a non-compliant process model into a compliant one. Sadiq et al. (2007) integrate control objectives in business processes using FCL. The approach classifies the control objectives among four types: flow, data, resource, and time tags (Sadiq et al. 2007). Mueller (2010) focuses on the structural analysis of BPMN process models by conceptualizing compliance requirements with the Process Pattern Modeling Language (PPML) and the Process Constraint Modeling Language (PCML). The modeling techniques facilitate the definition of structural model patterns and constraints, which are transformed into LTL in order to enable the formal analysis of BPMN models.

Woerzberger et al. (2008a, b) develop the visual Business Process Compliance Language (BPCL), which enables the definition of a limited set of control flow constraints on simplified syntax Business Process Execution Language (SimBPEL) process models, which are restricted to Web Service Business Process Execution Language (WS-BPEL) models (Alves et al. 2007). Accorsi et al. (2011) present an approach to verify data security requirements in cloud-based workflows, which is based on Petri-nets. They argue for a better comprehensibility of Petri-nets for business experts compared to other formal languages, such as LTL or FCL.

Ghose and Koliadis (2007) develop an approach that can be applied for generating process models and for selecting the most similar one to a given (compliant) process model. The approach aims to support the selection of process models that resolves compliance violations. Schumm et al. (2010) also supports the design of compliant business processes. Their approach uses pre-defined compliance fragments in order to support process modelers in creating compliant process models. For supporting root cause analyses, Elgammal et al. (2010) present a set of predefined composed compliance patterns. Combined with an analysis approach based on LTL, these patterns are used to guide process modelers in resolving compliance violations in business processes.

The Process Entailment from the Elicitation of Obligations and Permissions (PENELOPE) approach (Goedertier and Vanthienen 2006) provides the foundation for an automatic generation of compliant BPMN models using a Prolog algorithm. The approach allows for defining temporal restrictions as well as activity operators. Kuester et al. (2007) developed an approach that generates compliant business process models considering object life cycles, which contain all possible states of a data object, such as generated, granted, settled, and rejected for a credit application.

2.4.3 Run-Time Compliance Checking Approaches

Run-time compliance checking approaches differ from design-time compliance checking in their dependency on the business process execution environment. They require run-time information while executing a processes instance (Rossak et al. 2006). Liu et al. (2007) developed a modeling technique to represent compliance requirements, the so-called Business Property Specification Language (BPSL). The language affords a checking of compliance rules based on a Finite State Machine (FSM). For transforming models developed using the Business Process Execution Language (BPEL) into FSMs and checking them, the LTL and the Pi calculus (Milner 1999) was applied. Milosevic (2005) integrates policy definitions into business processes and enable the monitoring of run-time compliance.

One research stream of run-time compliance checking focuses on the analysis of business contract constraints in business processes (e.g., Alberti et al. 2007; Milosevic et al. 2002; Weigand and van den Heuvel 2002). Alberti et al. (2007) conceptualize contract constraints using three event notions: happened, expected, and not-expected. At run-time the approach records all events and checks whether or not contract conditions have been violated. Milosevic et al. (2002) present control mechanisms for a role-based contract management architecture and provide an assessment approach based on subjective logic. Weigand and van den Heuvel (2002) link the specification of business object-based workflow systems with the formal specification of business contract constraints, using the XML-based business contract specification language.

Ly et al. (2008; 2006) develop an approach for checking the semantic correctness in process instances at run-time. Limitations are discussed in Ly et al. (2012). Based on these limitations, they present a compliance-checking framework that enables visual compliance rule modeling and a subsequent automatic formalization using first-order predicate logic. The authors extend their approach to support the compliance of the whole lifecycle of business processes, which comprises compliance verification during design-time and run-time as well as for process changes and process evolutions (Ly et al. 2012).

2.4.4 Backward Compliance Checking

Approaches for backward compliance check whether a business process has been executed in accordance with all regulatory requirements and business constraints. To check the process instances, process execution logs are analyzed by using mining techniques (El Kharbili et al. 2008b). Van der Aalst et al. (2005) use an LTL checker to verify process logs regarding expected and unexpected behavior. Rozinat and van der Aalst (2008) extend this approach and check whether a process log complies with its process model. Chesani et al. (2007) develop an algorithm to transform process models of the health care industry into a formal language based computational logic and verify its conformance with a given process execution, derived from the event log. Ramezani et al. (2012) apply a Petri-net based approach to formalize 55 control flow oriented compliance constraints and classify them among 15 compliance rule categories.

Summing it up, compliance-checking approaches support the checking of business processes and provide a feedback whether the execution of a business process is in line with regulatory requirements. When the compliance of supervisory reports needs to be ensured, such approaches have a limited applicability. Supervisory reports are data-driven and receive its content mostly from data warehouses, whose development foundations are elaborated in the next section.

2.5 Data Warehouse Development

"A data warehouse is an integrated and timevarying collection of data derived from operational data and primarily used in strategic decision making by means of online analytical processing (OLAP) techniques" (Hüsemann et al. 2000, p. 1). It connects Online Transaction Processing (OLTP) systems with OLAP components (Chaudhuri and Umeshwar 1997).[1] The latter allow for a fast interactive navigation through the so-called multidimensional data space and supports information searches, mainly performed by managers (Colliat 1996). The tasks of extracting (E), transforming (T) and loading (L) data from the transactional systems into the data warehouse is called ETL process (Inmon 1996).

2.5.1 Data Warehouse Concepts

In order to conceptually design data warehouses, Holten (2003) specifies master data of management views. This master data contains concepts that are frequently used in data warehouse projects. Figure 2.2 summarizes common concepts (in the following, concepts are written in italics) and presents their representation in four different modeling techniques for conceptual data warehouse design, namely Multidimensional Entity Relationship Modeling (ME/RM) (Sapia et al. 1998), Application Design for Processing Technologies (ADAPT) (Bulos 1996), the Dimensional Fact Model (DFM) (Golfarelli et al. 1998) and H2 for Reporting (H2fR) (Becker et al. 2007d). Hettler et al. (2003) and Knackstedt et al. (2005) compare these modeling techniques and discuss their similarities and differences.

---

[1] For an overview of data warehouse and OLAP technologies see Chaudhuri and Umeshwar (1997).

Concept	ME/RM	ADAPT	DFM	H2fR
Dimension	-	Hierarchy	-	Dimension
Dimension Object	-	Dimension Member	-	Instance object
Hierarchy Level	Dimension Level Entity Type	Level	Dimension Attribute	Selection Object
Dimension Scope	-	Scope	-	Dimension Scope
Ratio	Attribut	Dimension Member	Fact Attribute (Measure)	Ratio
Ratio System	-	Measure Dimension	-	Ratio system
Information Object	Fact Relation-ship Type	Hypercube	Fact	Cube

Fig. 2.2 Comparison of data warehouse modeling concepts. Adapted from Knackstedt et al. (2005)

The first data warehouse concept is the *dimension*, which spans a multidimensional space for management views. Each dimension contains *dimension objects*, which represent concrete objects of interest, such as a concrete city or a concrete financial product. Dimension objects are organized in hierarchies, whereas each dimension object is uniquely assigned to one *hierarchy level*. In order to limit the navigation space of a dimension, the concept of *dimension scopes,* which are sub trees of a dimension, has been introduced. *Ratios* are hierarchically organized in *ratio systems* according to their functional or algebraic relationship. To define the (multidimensional) information space, consisting of one or more dimensions and ratios, the concept of *information objects* has been introduced (Holten 2003).

2.5.2 Data Warehouse Development Process

Traditional (transactional) database development processes usually comprise four phases: requirements analysis and specification, conceptual design, logical design, and physical design (Batini et al. 1992; Vossen 2008). These four phases are also identified as a process model for data warehouse design (Hüsemann et al. 2000, p. 1). The phases, their input and outputs as well as the phase results are depicted in Fig. 2.3. The *requirements analysis and specification phase* gets the operational databases and its schemas as input. The main objective of this phase is eliciting the user and business requirements for the data warehouse. A first impression of dimensions, attributes, and ratios is expressed and linked to database attributes of the operational databases.

The resulting semiformal business concept acts as input for the *conceptual design phase*, in which multidimensional data warehouse schemas are developed. The conceptual design phase aims to develop graphical multidimensional

Fig. 2.3 Process model for
data warehouse design.
Adapted from Hüsemann
et al. (2000)

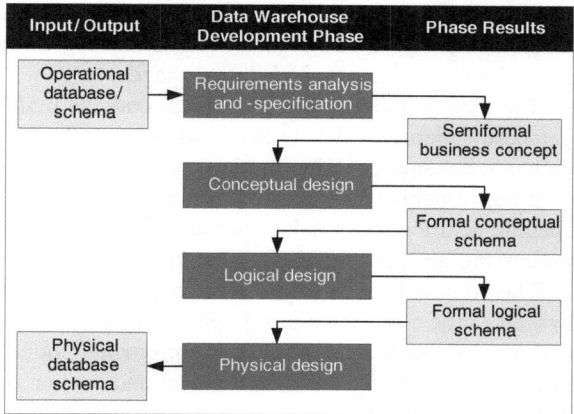

diagrams, containing dimensions, hierarchies, and ratios. Therefore, conceptual
modeling techniques help to conceptualize the data warehouse schema. According
to Rizzi et al. (2006), conceptual modeling techniques can be classified into three
categories: extensions to the entity relationship model (ERM) (e.g., Goeken and
Knackstedt 2009a; Sapia et al. 1998; Tryfona et al. 1999), extensions to UML
(e.g., Abelló et al. 2006; Harren and Herden 1999; Priebe and Pernul 2001), and
ad hoc models (e.g., Bulos 1996; Golfarelli et al. 1998).

In order to improve and accelerate the data warehouse design process, conceptual
reference models for data warehousing have been introduced (e.g., Becker and
Knackstedt 2003; Becker and Knackstedt 2004; Goeken 2004; Goeken and
Knackstedt 2007). Reference models are information models whose content can be
reused for several application scenarios (Becker and Knackstedt 2004; Fettke and
Loos 2007a; Thomas 2007; vom Brocke 2002). Regarding the conceptual data
warehouse development phase, reference models can be used to predefine dimensions, hierarchies, and ratios for a certain group of data warehouse users. The
configuration and adaptation of reference models allow for specifying parameters to
develop configurable reference models, which are reference models that can be
adapted to a company-specific environment (Knackstedt and Klose 2005).

The developed conceptual model of a data warehouse is used as an input for the
logical design phase. Based on the conceptual models, platform dependent models
of the data warehouse are developed that consider the logical structure of the data
warehouse (mostly relational). The logical model is constrained, for example, by
required response time or disc space, and is tailored for the implementation on the
target system (Rizzi et al. 2006). Target database systems are typically relational
or multidimensional. For relational database systems, the star or snowflake schemas, which differ in their way of normalization, are applied (Vassiliadis and Sellis
1999). A star schema's dimension tables are denormalized, while a snowflake
schema's dimension tables are normalized according to the different hierarchy
levels. Multidimensional databases are implemented by using data cube storage

procedures, such as condensed cubes, dwarfs, and QC-trees (Rizzi et al. 2006). The result of the logical design phase is a formal logical schema, which simultaneously is the input for the physical design stage.

The data warehouse design process ends with an implementation of a physical database schema, which is the result of the *physical design phase*. The physical database schema contains implementation specific and mostly performance relevant adjustments, such as partition and index considerations. In addition, OLAP-specific justifications, such as pre-aggregation of data and justifications for parallel processing are performed (Bellatreche and Mohania 2009; Rizzi et al. 2006).

The book at hand focuses on the requirements analysis and -specification phase as well as the conceptual design phase. The investigation of the collaboration of IS and legal experts addresses the requirements elicitation and stakeholder collaboration in IS projects. The development and evaluation of a modeling technique for conceptual regulatory reporting requirements addresses the conceptual data warehouse design phase.

2.6 Multisensory Law and Legal Visualization

Multisensory law is a new legal discipline and focuses on the investigation of sensory phenomena of the law, such as visual, audiovisual, or tactile-kinesthetic (Brunschwig 2012). "Multisensory law mainly deals with the law as a uni-and multisensory phenomenon within and outside the legal context" (Brunschwig 2012, p. 714). The major goal of multisensory law is to improve the communication and mediation of legal requirements. One area, which commonly uses legal visualization, is the traffic law. The famous stop sign, for example, signals a car driver that he has to stop at the end of the street in order to look whether the crossing street is free of traffic.

Legal visualization is a sub area of multisensory law and comprises the visual representation of legal requirements. Its history reaches back to the year 1300, where the Saxon Mirror (ger. "Sachsenspiegel") was introduced to illustrate the law in pictures, sequences of images, and texts (Oppitz 1990). Today, graphic designers, psychologists, lawyers, and experts from related disciplines again try to visualize the law by using models or other graphical representations (Sachs-Hombach 2005). Boehme-Neßler (2005), for example, discusses the opportunities and threats of legal visualization and argues for the potential of visualization approaches for the understanding of legal requirements.

Nowadays, legal visualization approaches focus on a more structured representation of legal requirements. The usage of mind mapping for the representation of legal information on E-government websites, for example, is investigated by Brunschwig (2006). As a mediation device between lawyers and client's, McCloskey (1998) introduce the concept of legal map making, which comprises two approaches. The first one is called organizing metaphors and comprises images, such as a bridge or a scale to visualizing legal requirements. The second approach is the template approach, which comprises the drawing of cases and the extraction of essential legal elements, which are reused to develop a logical model to explain the case (McCloskey 1998).

A second research stream focuses on the visualization of contracts (Becker et al. 2012f; Berger-Walliser et al. 2011; Kabilan 2005). Becker et al. (2012f) argue for the usage of conceptual process models for the representation of procedural parts of a contract. Berger-Walliser et al. (2011) suggest to use contractual literacy and visualization in order to help establishing a cross-professional communication among business and legal experts. Kabilan (2005) discusses the transformation of contract obligations to BPMN models and argues for the need to semantically integrate contract terms and conditions into business process models.

A third research stream, which is more process model related, focuses on the integration of legal requirements and control objectives in modeling techniques (Alpar and Olbrich 2005; Carnaghan 2006; Olbrich and Simon 2008; Sadiq et al. 2007). Alpar and Olbrich (2005) extend the event-driven process chains by legal aspects to explicating the regulatory requirements for a certain event or activity. They argue for the relevance of including the legal framework in process models and demonstrate the modeling technique with a process example of the German Federal Insurance Institute for Salaried Employees. Olbrich and Simon (2008) discuss the formal modeling of regulations for regulated processes in public administrations. The developed approach allows for deriving process structures, which are implicitly described in the legal paragraphs. Carnaghan (2006) investigated business process modeling approaches for its usefulness for audit risk assessments. The modeling constructs of different business process modeling techniques are compared to those identified as relevant for process level audit risk assessments (Carnaghan 2006). Sadiq et al. (2007) argue for the need to provide a systematic approach that helps understanding business and control objectives of business processes. They visualize four types of control tags: flow (control flow constraints), data (data retention and lineage requirements), resource (access, role, and authorization management), and time tags (deadlines and maximum durations) and annotate them to process model elements (Sadiq et al. 2007).

This book addresses multisensory law and legal visualization in two ways. First, the developed modeling technique for regulatory reporting requirements is a contribution to the field of legal visualization since the law is represented in a structured graphical way. Second, the visual representation of the business process compliance patterns is perceived as a transfer of legal requirements into a structural pattern, which can also be regarded as a legal visualization.

2.7 Regulatory Requirements Engineering

In order to conceptualize regulatory requirements for the sake of developing compliant IS, two major challenges exist. First, compliance experts and IS developers must determine the set of regulatory requirements that are relevant for business processes and IT systems. Second, tasks that result from the regulatory requirements must be determined in order to comply with the regulations (Kerrigan and Law 2003). Thus, an organization must first identify all relevant regulations before it begins to check whether or not an IT system is compliant with regulatory requirements (Otto and Antón 2007). But even if the relevant requirements are identified, it is still challenging to extract requirements for system design because the legal terms and expressions are difficult to understand for IS designers and non-legal experts (Toval et al. 2002).

Systems for supporting legal requirements in requirements engineering are faced with several challenges. Otto and Antón (2007) identify nine elements for systems that support the regulatory-driven analysis and requirement specification. They guide the development of the business process and reporting compliance artifacts in this book. According to Otto and Antón (2007), such systems must allow for:

- identifying relevant regulations
- classification of regulations with meta data
- prioritizing of regulations and exceptions
- managing evolving regulations
- tracing between references and requirements
- ensuring consistency by using data dictionaries and glossaries
- navigating and searching semi-automatically
- annotating regulatory statements
- computing queries for comparing legal concepts and compliance.

According to Massey et al. (2012), research in legal requirements engineering focuses on two streams: techniques that derive legal requirements for software (e.g., Barth et al. 2006; Massacci et al. 2005) and techniques that ensure the compliance of software requirements with regulations (e.g., Breaux and Antón 2008; Breaux et al. 2006; Otto and Antón 2007). This book addresses both streams. On the one hand, a modeling technique to represent legal supervisory requirements is presented, which helps ensuring the compliance of reporting systems (Becker et al. 2011a; Becker et al. 2012a; Becker et al. 2012e). On the other hand, an approach to check the compliance of business processes and conceptual data warehouse models automatically is presented and evaluated (Becker et al. 2012b,d; Eggert et al. 2013a).

This section provides the foundations to develop new and extended artifacts in order to manage the compliance of information systems and business processes. Basic regulatory requirements in the financial service industry and their impact on business processes and the data warehouse are introduced. Related work in the area of business process modeling and process compliance analysis builds the foundation for the development of a new compliance analysis approach for business processes. The data warehouse development process is described in order to explicate the necessity of conceptual data warehouse modeling. Finally, legal visualization and regulatory requirements engineering works are elaborated in order to provide the foundations for the development of a modeling technique for regulatory requirements.

Chapter 3
Research Design

3.1 Design Science Research

The IS research discipline is characterized by two major research paradigms: behavioral science and design science (Hevner et al. 2004). While behavioral science aims to develop and evaluate theories regarding the behavior of humans and organizations, design science aims to develop new and innovative artifacts (Hevner et al. 2004; March and Smith 1995; Winter 2008). The research work at hand predominantly follows the design science research paradigm (Peffers et al. 2007) for structuring the research process.

Several different research results have been developed in this work in order to address research questions RQ1–RQ4. Research results that follow the design science research paradigm can be classified within the research output schema of March and Smith (1995), who develop a classification of relevant design science artifacts. These research outputs are constructs, models, methods, and instantiations (March and Smith 1995). *Constructs* form a specialized language and explicate the shared knowledge of a particular domain, such as the mentioned modeling techniques for business processes (Keller et al. 1992; Object Management Group 2005; Object Management Group 2006) or data warehouses (Becker et al. 2007d; Bulos 1996; Golfarelli et al. 1998; Sapia et al. 1998). "A model is a set of propositions or statements expressing relationships among constructs" (March and Smith 1995, p. 256). Applying BPMN to develop a concrete business process model is one example for a model artifact. A *method* comprises a set of steps that are used to perform a special task. Methods make use of constructs and models and represent tasks for working with these artifacts, such as transforming models from one representation to another one. Finally, *instantiations* realize and implement one or more artifact(s) either as a specific tool or as an information system (March and Smith 1995).

Based on design research and research about design research, Peffers et al. (2007) developed a process model that guides rigorous and relevant design science research. The design science research methodology (DSRM) consists of six partly

M. Eggert, *Compliance Management in Financial Industries*,
SpringerBriefs in Information Systems, DOI: 10.1007/978-3-319-03913-8_3,
© The Author(s) 2014

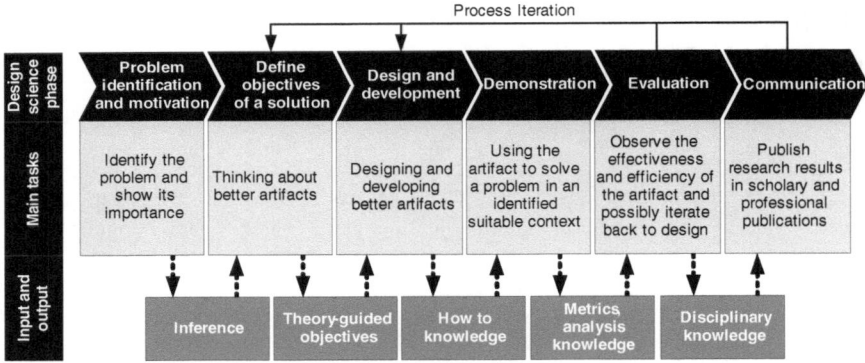

Fig. 3.1 Design science research methodology. Adapted from Peffers et al. (2007)

iterative phases, which are depicted in Fig. 3.1. In the following, the main tasks of the six phases and its inputs and outputs are briefly explained in accordance to Peffers et al. (2007).

- *Problem identification and motivation*: The first phase in the design science process aims to identify and conceptualize the problem and evaluates the value of a solution. By conceptually atomizing the problem, a possible solution loses complexity and the problem becomes manageable. Expressing the value of a solution to the problem at hand motivates researchers to work on a problem solution. As a result, inferences for a possible solution are derived.
- *Define the objectives of a solution*: Based on the identified problem and research motivation, the second phase aims at defining the objectives of a solution, which might be quantitative (e.g., the performance of the algorithm should be increased by 10 %) or qualitative (e.g., the usability of the interface must be improved). Fulfilling this phase requires fundamental knowledge of the current state of the problem, the current state of the solution, and the efficiency of the solution. The results of this phase are theory-guided objectives, which can be applied for the solution development.
- *Design and development*: Aiming to design and develop artifacts that comprise solutions for the identified problem (constructs, models, methods, and instantiations), the third phase includes the determination of the functionality and architecture of the solution to be developed. Thereby, knowledge to solve the identified problem is generated, which acts as input for the demonstration phase.
- *Demonstration*: The goal of the demonstration phase is to prove that the idea for solving the identified problem works. This is facilitated by showing that the developed solution can be used to solve one or more instances of the described problem. Several different research methods can be applied for this research step, such as case studies, simulations, or experiments. The results of this phase are metrics and analyses, which provide knowledge about the applicability of the developed solution.

- *Evaluation*: Compared to the demonstration phase, the evaluation phase aims to measure how well the developed artifact works for solving the identified problem. One essential task within the evaluation is the comparison of the observed application results with the former defined objectives of a solution. The evaluation can comprise different methods to get appropriate empirical evidence or logical proof that the designed artifact is a proper solution to the identified problem. Depending on the results, the researcher may go back to the design phase in order to find a different solution to the problem.
- *Communication*: Hevner et al. (2004) and Archer (1984) argue for the need to communicate research results. This last step in the design science research process comprises the continuous publication of research results in scholarly and professional journals and conferences. Therefore, knowledge about the scientific discipline and relevant outlets is necessary.

3.2 Complementary Research Methods

A research method consists of a couple of sequential operations that acquire knowledge and lead to predictable results (Iivari et al. 1998; Mingers 2001). Mingers (2001) argues for the desirability of applying a multi-method approach in IS research. Applying a pluralist methodology in IS research has two major advantages. First, the plurality of structures in the real world makes it necessary to analyze the generated events with different methods. Second, research is not seen as a single event. Rather, research work is perceived as a process containing different tasks and problems, which require different methods (Mingers 2001). Many IS researchers follow this methodology pluralism (e.g., Hevner et al. 2004; Iivari et al. 1998; Peffers et al. 2007).

Each research result presented in this book has been developed by applying one or more research methods, which are briefly described in the following. Common research methods in IS research are interviews and focus group interviews, informed arguments, literature reviews, method engineering, surveys, laboratory experiments, and case studies. They are applied and discussed in several IS research papers (e.g., Boudreau et al. 2001; Chen and Hirschheim 2004; Iivari et al. 1998; Mingers 2001; Rosemann and Vessey 2008; Vessey et al. 2002). In the following, each complementary research method, which is applied in this work, is briefly described.

- An *interview* is not simply an exchange of questions and their corresponding answers. Rather, an interview is a process, in which two or more persons are actively involved and which leads to the creation of a collaborative effort to creating a contextually bound story (Fontana and Frey 2005). The interview process is controlled by the researcher and can be conducted as one-to-one or as a group interview (Oates 2006). An interview process can be structured or unstructured. Structured interviews are guided by a question guideline, whereas unstructured interviews constantly react to the interview flow without a clear question structure. Data from interviews can be collected in three ways, either by making field notes of what the interview partner says or by using audio or video tape recording, followed by a transcription (Oates 2006). A special kind of interview is the group interview, also called *focus group interview* (Kvale 1996; Oates 2006). Focus groups use group interaction as one major part of the method. A common group size is between 8 and 12 individuals plus a moderator, who promotes the discussion and ensures that the discussion focuses on the topic of interest (Stewart et al. 2007). Independent of the concrete interview type, the method must be used carefully because of several biases, such as socially desirable responding (Podsakoff et al. 2003), which may hinder a proper research process.

- *Informed arguments* belong to the descriptive evaluation methods and make use of information from an existing knowledge base and derive convincing arguments for the usefulness of artifacts (Hevner et al. 2004). "Argument is a means of discovering truth, negotiating differences, and solving problems" (Yagelski and Miller 2012, p. 2). To create an informed argument, often patterns of logic, particularly for inductive and deductive reasoning, are applied. Hevner et al. (2004) suggest to use informed arguments as a means to evaluate IS research artifacts.

- A *literature review* is the backbone of each scientific work and provides a foundation for advancing the knowledge base (vom Brocke et al. 2009; Webster and Watson 2002). Rowley and Slack (2004) define a literature review as "a summary of a subject field that supports the identification of specific research questions" (Rowley and Slack 2004, p. 31). Several procedures for conducting literature reviews have been suggested in the IS literature (e.g., Fettke 2006; vom Brocke et al. 2009; Webster and Watson 2002). They all have in common that they suggest to use a structured forward and backward search after an initial search process has been conducted. In this way, the whole body of knowledge is investigated and it can be ensured that all relevant research works for one topic are considered in the literature review. The goal of each literature review is not only to provide information about the past research. Rather it should endup in a research agenda, which can be used to close the identified research gaps (vom Brocke et al. 2009). Reviews do not necessarily focus on scholarly journals and conference proceedings. They may also be applied for analyzing newspaper articles or online reports.

- In order to develop IS design methods, the concept of *method engineering* (ME) has been introduced (Brinkkemper 1996; Brinkkemper et al. 1999). "Method engineering is the engineering discipline to design, construct and adapt methods, techniques and tools for the development of information systems" (Brinkkemper 1996, p. 276). It is closely related to situational method engineering, which aims to develop project-specific methods, derived from other method fragments (Harmsen et al. 1994). One example is the adaptation or extension of a general data modeling technique, such as the ERM, to a special project context. Both method engineering and situational method engineering aim to formalize the usage of methods for system development (Henderson-Sellers and Ralyté 2010). Ralyté et al. (2004) distinguish four ME types. While ad hoc ME approaches start developing a method from scratch, paradigm-based ME approaches build upon existing models or meta-models to instantiate, abstract or adapt them to develop new To-Be models. Extension-based ME approaches extend existing methods and enhance these methods with new constructs. Assembly-based ME use method fragments in order to recreate a new method. Therefore, the concept of method components is used (Ralyté et al. 2004).

- A *survey* is a means to elicit characteristics, actions, or opinions of a large group of people (Tanur 1982). According to Pinsonneault and Kraemer (1993), a survey for research purposes has three characteristics. First, the survey produces quantitative aspects of the investigated population. Since the survey method belongs to the group of quantitative research methods, standardized information about the subjects are necessary. Second, the main way of collecting data is the usage of questionnaires with standardized questions. The questions of such questionnaires might be about the respondent himself or about other analysis objects. Third, in general, data is collected about a fraction of the whole population, a so-called sample. The sample should be large enough to allow for statistically significant analyses (Pinsonneault and Kraemer 1993). Conducting a survey requires the consideration of some guidelines for preventing a bias of respondents. Several guidelines to prepare questionnaires have been published so far. The development of questionnaires in this work is guided by the work of Dillmann et al. (2009).

- Experiments in a controlled environment are used in order to validate IS research artifacts. The so called *laboratory experiments* take place in a setting, whose variables and assignments of participants to various treatments are controlled by the researcher (Boudreau et al. 2001). Vessey et al. (2002) differentiate laboratory experiments in experiments with human subjects and software experiments. Whereas experiments that include human subjects focus on the observation of problem-solving situations, software experiments are characterized by the comparison of one or more systems based on various dimensions (Vessey et al. 2002). This book focuses on laboratory experiments with human subjects.

- A *case study* "examines a phenomenon in its natural setting, employing multiple methods of data collection to gather information from one or a few entities (people, groups, or organizations)" (Benbasat et al. 1987, p. 370). It is conducted in the field (e.g., at a company's headquarter, office, or branch) and can also be described as a field study (Chen and Hirschheim 2004). A case study makes use of several data collection methods, such as sighting documents, conducting interviews, physical artifacts (devices, tools, etc.) or observing the field environment (Benbasat et al. 1987; Yin 2003). Yin (2003) differentiates six types of case studies. Single and multiple case studies refer to the number of cases they observe. Both types can be combined with the primary character of the case study, which can be exploratory, descriptive, and explanatory. Case studies are applied in different disciplines, such as accounting (Scapens 1990) or operations management (McCutcheon and Meredith 1993). In IS research, case studies are one of the most applied research methods (Chen and Hirschheim 2004; Orlikowski and Baroudi 1991). According to Benbasat et al. (1987) the application of case studies for IS research has three advantages. First, the usage of IS can be investigated in a natural setting, which enables gathering new insights into practice and the generation of theories from practice. Second, the understanding of phenomena can be increased by its observation. Third, case studies can be used to investigate areas, which are currently not attended in IS research. New industry-relevant topics may arise, which are currently not regarded in research. Case studies provide valuable insights into such topics and investigation areas (Benbasat et al. 1987).

3.3 Research Process and Outcome

As outlined in Sect. 1.2, this book has four major research questions (RQ1–RQ4). Each question is answered by two or more research results, which are assigned to one of the four research areas (Compliance Management and IS, Business Process Compliance, Reporting Compliance, and Collaboration of IS and Legal Experts). Furthermore, each research result can be primarily assigned to one or more phases of the design science research methodology according to Peffers et al. (2007). Error! Reference source not found. depicts the assignment of each research result to its primarily addressed DSRM phases, and the applied research method(s). In the following, each research result, its applied research method, and its primarily affected DSRM phase is briefly outlined.

3.3.1 Compliance Management and Information Systems

The results in the first research area address the investigation of the impact of regulation on conceptual IS design (RQ1). First, the influence of regulation on the organization of IT departments and IT service providers is investigated by conducting a survey (Eggert et al. 2013b). A cross-industry study using Structural Equation Modeling (SEM) and Partial Least Squares (PLS) based on Contingency Theory (Donaldson 2001) is presented. Based on informed arguments, a research framework for model-based compliance management artifacts is developed (Becker et al. 2012c). Both research works can be primarily assigned to the problem identification and objective definition phases of the DSRM.

3.3.2 Business Process Compliance

The second block aims at improving the efficiency of business process compliance checking (RQ2). Therefore, an extensive literature review is conducted in order to identify research gaps in the state-of-the-art of business process compliance checking approaches (Becker et al. 2012a). Based on these findings, the design and development of a business process model checking approach that (1) is applicable on arbitrary modeling techniques and (2) for all kinds of compliance requirements (expressed as compliance patterns) is presented (Becker et al. 2011a). Further, the approach is demonstrated as a tool implementation. Based on the developed business process model checking approach, an evaluation method for compliance checking approaches, which partly applies considerations of the Technology Acceptance Model (TAM) (Davis et al. 1989; Venkatesh and Bala 2008) is presented (Becker et al. 2012e). The method is mainly discussed by informed arguments and can be assigned to the evaluation phase of the DSRM. Finally, the development process of the generalizable business process compliance checking approach plus a focus group interview-based evaluation at an IT service provider for financial institutes is discussed.

3.3.3 Reporting Compliance

The central goal of the research work in the reporting compliance section is to improve the modeling and analysis of regulatory report requirements (RQ3). First, the challenges of regulatory reporting for IS engineering are derived from two focus group interviews with experts from the financial industry. These qualitative results are matched with results from a structured literature review, which has led to a research agenda. In order to model regulatory reporting requirements for bank supervision, a multidimensional conceptual modeling technique is developed using method engineering and informed arguments. The modeling technique is evaluated with a laboratory experiment (Eggert et al. 2013a). In order to demonstrate the applicability of the modeling technique it is implemented into an adapted modeling tool based on the H2-Toolset (Fleischer 2013) (Becker et al. 2012d). The research work primarily makes use of a method engineering approach and informed arguments to express the relevance of the tool extensions for conceptual report analyses. It can be assigned to the DSRM phases design, development, and demonstration. Finally, the modeling technique is applied in three modeling projects for regulatory report requirements. In a laboratory experiment, students developed three extensive data warehouse models based on the modeling technique in order to demonstrate its feasibility (Becker et al. 2012b).

3.3.4 Collaboration of IS and Legal Experts

The overall research objective of the fourth research area is to conceptualize and to support the collaboration of IS and legal experts (RQ4). Three research artifacts have been developed in this area. A model-based framework for the collaboration of IS and legal experts in regulatory-driven IS projects provides insights into the practitioner perception of IS and law (Knackstedt et al. 2012). Based on a case study of an e-government case in Germany, the framework was developed and has led to design guidelines for further IS projects in a regulatory context. The relationship of IS research and law is then investigated in order to motivate a combined perspective in further IS research projects (Knackstedt et al. 2013). Based on an extensive literature review and informed arguments, the perceived relationship of IS and law is elaborated and discussed. Finally, the development of a research portal for legal informatics and information law provides a means for collaboration and for identifying research works in this evolving discipline (Knackstedt et al. 2010). Based on the informed argument approach, the portal is introduced and demonstrated.

Chapter 4
Research Results

4.1 Compliance Management and Information Systems

Revisiting a model-based perspective on compliance management enforces the necessity to identify the relevance of models and its analysis for the purpose of managing regulatory requirements for IS. Following the first research question, this section aims to investigate the influence of regulation on model-based information system design (RQ1). This research objective is fulfilled by investigating the influence of regulation on the organization and management of IS (Eggert et al. 2013b). Furthermore, the results motivate the development of a classification framework for model-based research artifacts for compliance management (Becker et al. 2012c).

Based on the contingency theory (Galbraith 1973; Lawrence and Lorsch 1967) and its adaptation for Management Information Systems (MIS) (Weill and Olson 1989), a theory-based framework for the influence of regulation on the management and organization of IT departments has been developed (Becker et al. 2011b). In this context, the term MIS is used for all organizational capabilities of an IT department or IT service provider. The model acts as a theoretical basis to determine the influence of the degree of regulation on the management and organization of MIS (RQ1.1). The basic assumption thereby is that the more an organization is regulated the more legal experts are involved in IT projects (hypothesis H1). Clark and Brennan (1996) stated that the more complex the social and physical world is, the more complex is the establishment of a common ground. Particularly in regulatory-driven IT projects, legal and IS experts are faced with communication challenges caused by different educational background and a different language.

Conceptual models help establishing a common ground between stakeholders (Kung and Sölvberg 1986; Mylopoulos 1992). This leads to the second hypothesis: More involvement of compliance experts in IS development projects leads to an increased use of formal design and analysis approaches (hypothesis H2). Further, it is assumed that the use of models and model analysis methods has a positive influence on the performance of MIS, such as software development process quality.

M. Eggert, *Compliance Management in Financial Industries*,
SpringerBriefs in Information Systems, DOI: 10.1007/978-3-319-03913-8_4,
© The Author(s) 2014

Table 4.1 Respondent demographics

Title	Senior managers	Middle managers	Advisors	Total
N	25	61	19	105
Percentage (%)	23.81	58.10	18.09	100
Work experience (SD) (years)	18.52 (9.05)	18.80 (9.95)	12.42 (10.00)	18.44 (9.94)

The theoretical model was applied in order to develop a survey that has been used to ask IT and compliance experts from the retail and banking industry as well as from governmental institutions. The questionnaire can be found in Eggert et al. (2013b). Altogether 105 full answered questionnaires could be collected at two German practitioner conferences and through an online and paper based survey. Table 4.1 provides an overview about the skill and work experience level of the respondents. All participants have an average work experience of about 18 years with a standard deviation of 9.94 years. The demographics indicate that the majority of respondents are highly experienced.

The data was analyzed using the SEM/PLS method and the software smartPLS (Ringle et al. 2005). Except for two hypotheses (the relationship between the degree of regulation and the usage of formalization and analysis as well as the relationship between expert involvement and process quality), all remaining hypotheses could be confirmed. In particular, the confirmation of a strong relationship between the degree of regulation and the involvement of compliance experts in regulatory-driven IT projects (H1) motivate further research about the way of collaboration.

Furthermore, a positive correlation between the involvement of compliance experts and the usage of formalized modeling and analysis methods could be confirmed (H2). This significant correlation indicates that the more compliance experts are involved in regulatory IT projects the higher is the probability of using model and model analysis approaches in such projects. These results accumulate the basis for the thesis at hand, as they indicate that conceptual models and analysis approaches play a significant role in regulatory-driven IT projects. The whole model, the R^2, Q^2, and beta values are depicted in Fig. 4.1. The model contains seven constructs and one control variable. A significant correlation could be found between the degree of regulation and the expert involvement (H1). The more an organization is regulated the more compliance and legal experts work in regulatory-motivated IT projects. Furthermore, the data confirms a significant relationship between expert involvement and the usage of formalization and analysis methods, such as modeling techniques and model analysis approaches (H2).

Besides the confirmation of the hypotheses H1 and H2, the model reveals two more interesting insights into the impact of regulation on MIS. The significant correlation between executive commitment for regulatory IT compliance and the involvement of compliance experts (expert involvement) indicates that only when the management strongly supports IT compliance, corresponding legal and compliance experts are part of such IT projects. In turn, if executive commitment for IT compliance is missing, the likelihood of compliance and legal expert involvement in regulatory-driven IT-projects is much smaller.

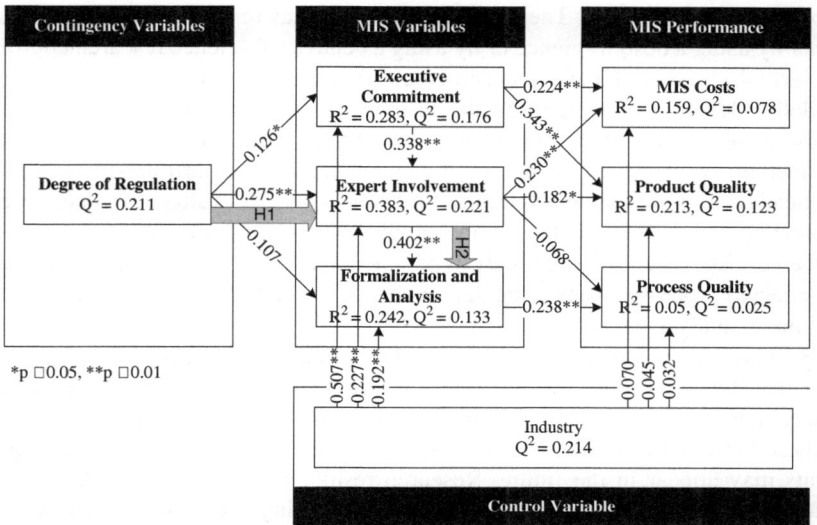

Fig. 4.1   The influence of regulation on MIS (Structural Model). Adapted from Eggert et al. (2013b)

Furthermore, the positive relationship between the usage of formalization and analysis methods and the outcome of software development processes (process quality) confirms a higher likelihood that regulatory IT projects will be finished in time and budget when modeling and analysis methods are applied. Due to experiences in non-regulatory IT projects, this result is not surprising, but again confirms the importance of models and analysis techniques for IT compliance projects.

4.1.1   Framework for Model-Based Compliance Management

The results above emphasize the necessity for using conceptual models and their analysis methods in regulatory-driven IT projects. While the alignment of IT with business requirements has been thoroughly investigated under the term IT alignment (e.g., Henderson and Venkatraman 1992; Parker et al. 1988), the alignment of IT with regulatory requirements has remained a less regarded field of study. Initial results on legal requirements engineering and the analysis and extraction of rules and obligations are provided by Otto and Antón (2007), Breaux and Antón (2008), and Breaux et al. (2006). In order to address this gap, a research framework for merging conceptual modeling and law for regulatory compliant IS design is developed (Becker et al. 2012c) (RQ1.2). The framework comprises three dimensions to classify corresponding research results. First, the research artifact is classified regarding the applied research method. The research result that has to be classified was created either by using a design science or by using a behavioral science research approach.

Second, the research artifacts can be classified among their model level. Three modeling levels are available in the framework: metamodel, model, and model analysis. While new modeling techniques and their evaluations can be assigned to the metamodel level, the model level contains all research artifacts regarding the application of a modeling technique to develop and to evaluate a concrete conceptual model, for example, a conceptual reference model for compliant bank processes. Approaches for the analysis of conceptual models, for example, regarding the effected processes when a regulation changes, and its evaluation are assigned to the model analysis level.

Finally, the third dimension classifies the model type or model domain, which describes the main purpose of the model. The dimension contains the domains process compliance, reporting compliance, and web applications but it is not limited to these three domains. Other domains of the model application for legal requirements may appear in the future. Research results regarding the regulatory compliance of business processes (e.g., Eshuis and Wieringa 2004; Ghose and Koliadis 2007; Goedertier and Vanthienen 2006; Governatori et al. 2008; Governatori and Rotolo 2010) can be assigned to the process compliance domain. Research about the regulatory alignment of IS in order to fulfill reporting requirements (e.g., Goeken and Knackstedt 2008, 2009b; Knackstedt et al. 2012) can be assigned to the reporting compliance domain. The consideration of legal requirements for web applications have been investigated by Knackstedt et al. (2006).

By applying the framework, existing research in the field of model-based compliance management can be classified and further research potential can be identified. For this research work, the framework is applied in order to classify the model-based research artifacts for reporting and business process compliance. The framework is depicted in Fig. 4.2 and contains all business process (results 3–6) and reporting compliance (results 7–10) research results developed in this book.

4.2 Business Process Compliance

The identified relevance of conceptual models for regulatory-driven IT projects indicates that business process models play a significant role for the regulatory-driven development and change of business processes. On the one hand the financial sector is one of the most regulated industry sectors (Abdullah et al. 2010), which hampers the checking of business processes for their compliance with rules and regulations. On the other hand a bank consists of several hundred business processes (Raduescu et al. 2006), for example, report on a financial institution with more than 1,800 business processes), which possibly may be affected by a regulatory change. In order to deal with this challenge, the research goal of business process compliance research is to improve the efficiency and effectiveness of business process compliance checking (RQ2).

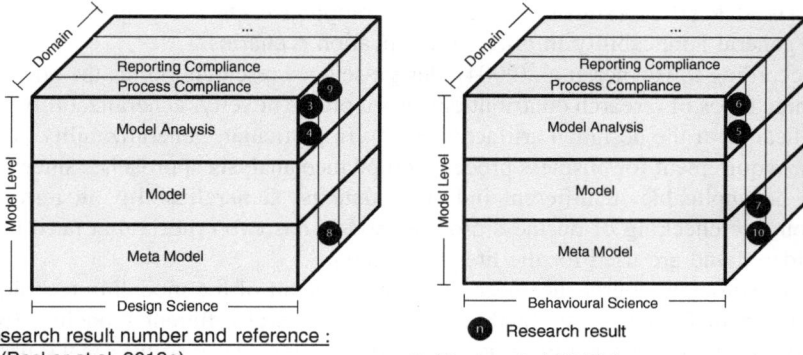

Research result number and reference :

3: (Becker et al. 2012a)
4: (Becker et al. 2011a)
8: (Eggert et al. 2013a)
9: (Becker et al. 2012d)

5: (Becker et al. 2012e)
6: Evaluation of the Compliance checking
   approach (Section 4.2)
7: Elicitation of challenges for regulatory driven
   requirements engineering (Section 4.3)
10: (Becker et al. 2012b)

Fig. 4.2   Research framework for legal information systems modeling. Adapted from Becker et al. (2012c)

Four aspects focusing on a conceptual design-time perspective address research question RQ2. First, a state of the art analysis about the existing compliance checking approaches and its general applicability is conducted (RQ2.1). The results are used for developing a compliance checking approach that addresses the identified research gap. The goal is to develop a business process analysis approach that is (a) general applicable and that (b) increases the compliance checking efficiency and effectiveness (RQ2.2). The developed artifact is implemented in a prototype in order to demonstrate the feasibility. In order to evaluate the artifact, an evaluation concept is developed that answers the question of how to evaluate a business process compliance checking approach in an industry case study (RQ2.3). The concept is then applied in two evaluation workshops. The workshop results provide insights into the relevance and acceptance of the developed generalizable compliance checking approach for financial industries (RQ2.4).

4.2.1 State-of-the-Art

Many business process compliance checking approaches have been introduced in the literature (Awad 2010; El Kharbili et al. 2008a). They can be classified regarding the point in time when the analysis is executed. In general, the approaches can be differentiated between forward (design-time and run-time) and backward compliance checking approaches (see Sect. 2.4). The state-of-the-art analysis at hand investigates design-time compliance checking approaches and their general applicability in different application scenarios.

According to Hevner et al. (2004), design-science research "holds the potential for three types of research contributions based on the novelty, generalizability, and significance of the designed artifact" (p. 87). In particular, generalizability is one major requirement for business process compliance analysis approaches since they must be applicable in different industry contexts. Generalizability in terms of compliance checking of business process models has two criteria that need to be considered and are used for the literature search.

First, sufficient approaches need to be independent of the modeling technique. According to Recker et al. (2009), there exist several different modeling techniques, which are frequently in use. In particular financial institutes make use of several different modeling techniques in order to model their business processes (Becker et al. 2010a). Thus, the first literature search criterion is the *modeling technique generalizability*. An approach has a high modeling technique generalizability when its application is not restricted to one single modeling technique and when no compiler is needed in order to transform a model for analysis.

The second literature search criterion is the *compliance rule generalizability*. Many different compliance rules and regulatory requirements exist, which need to be checked in business process models. A narrow compliance rule generalizability allows for checking linear control flows, such as predecessor-successor relationships. A medium compliance rule generalizability additionally allows for checking annotations, such as attributes of business process activities. Finally, a broad compliance rule generalizability has no limitations for the checking of business process models. Approaches that reach this state allow for checking all regulatory requirements regardless their complexity. In particular patterns across different models, such as process model, organizational chart, and IT architecture, are rated as rather complex compliance patterns.

In addition to these two analysis criteria, the practical applicability and evaluation of the approach is an important step in the design science research paradigm (Hevner et al. 2004). Three levels of evaluation are differentiated. The lowest level is the absence of any evaluation. Such approaches solely contain a technological concept and have had no proof-of-concept. The next level comprises approaches that have been implemented in a software tool. Approaches with the most advanced evaluation implement the concept as a prototype and apply the software in a realistic company case study.

Based on a structured literature search and by following the search principles of Webster and Watson (2002) as well as vom Brocke et al. (2009), 26 different relevant business process compliance checking approaches could be identified and evaluated (Becker et al. 2012a). Figure 4.3 depicts the relevant approaches and their classification between the two dimensions Modeling Language Generalizability and Compliance Rule Generalizability. A rectangle represents the absence of evaluation, a circle represents approaches with prototypal evaluation and a diamond stands for approaches with real world evaluation. All numbers refer to the approaches in Table 4.2.

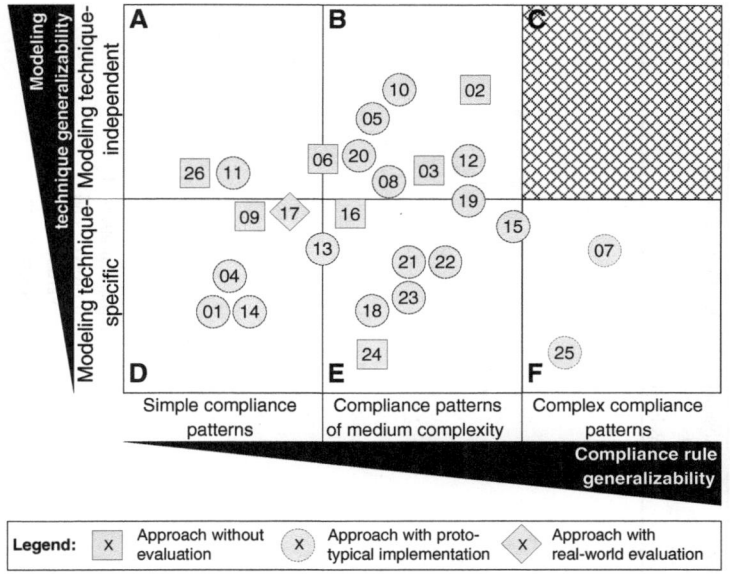

Fig. 4.3 Classification of compliance checking approaches (Becker et al. 2012a)

The results of the literature review show that current developments in the area of business process compliance checking either focus on specific modeling techniques (areas D, E, F) or cannot support the whole range of compliance patterns (areas A, B, D, E). Additionally, only one approach (Mueller 2010) (No. 17) could be identified, which was evaluated in an industry setting. Concluding the results, current business process compliance checking approaches are not able to support the generalizability in terms of modeling techniques and compliance rules. Thus, they lack in practical relevance, which demands for investigating new general applicable solutions for business process compliance checking (area C).

4.2.2 Model-Based Business Process Compliance Analysis Approach

The identified research gap is addressed by the development of a model-based business process compliance checking approach that is (a) applicable for all modeling techniques, (b) capable of checking all kinds of compliance patterns, and (c) is prototypically implemented in a meta modeling tool (Becker et al. 2011a). The approach makes use of set operations applied to a set of modeling language elements. Therefore, the approach operationalizes any conceptual model as a graph (G) with model elements as vertices (V) and its relationships as edges (E), where

Table 4.2 Compliance checking approaches

No.	Approach	Modeling language generalizability	Compliance rule generalizability			Evaluation		
			Simple	Medium complexity	Complex	Absence of evaluation	Against research gap	Against real-world
1	Quality constraints on business processes (Foerster et al. 2005, 2007)	UML activity diagrams	x	–	–	–	x	–
2	FCL/PCL-based approaches (Governatori and Milosevic 2006; Governatori et al. 2006; Governatori and Rotolo 2010; Hoffmann et al. 2009; Lu et al. 2008a, b)	Graph-(e.g., BPMN) and net-based languages (e.g., Petri nets)	x	x	–	x	–	–
3	Modeling control objectives (Sadiq et al. 2007)	Simple modeling language	x	x	–	x	–	–
4	Graphical BPCL (Woerzberger et al. 2008a, b)	SimBPCL	x	–	–	–	x	–
5	BPSL (Liu et al. 2007)	Exemplary discussion on BPEL (but OPAL also supports other modelling languages)	x	–	–	–	(Implementation of prototype and evaluation of performance)	–

(continued)

Table 4.2 (continued)

No.	Approach	Modeling language generalizability	Compliance rule generalizability			Evaluation		
			Simple	Medium complexity	Complex	Absence of evaluation	Against research gap	Against real-world
6	Resource-related compliance rules in Prolog (Kumar and Liu 2008)	Standard workflow patterns	(x)	(Organization)	–	x	–	–
7	Validation of flow conditions using model checker (Monakova et al. 2009)	BPEL	x	(Conditional control flow)	x	–	x	–
8	BPMN-Q queries, anti-patterns and violation resolution (Awad 2007, 2010; Awad et al. 2008, 2009a, b; Awad and Weske 2010)	BPMN (no full support of all constructs), authors argue that concept is generic and can be applied to other modelling languages	x	(Data)	–	–	x (Implementation of prototype, demonstration using constructed scenario)	–
9	Pattern-based violation detection and automated resolution (Ghose and Koliadis 2007)	BPMN	x	–	–	x	–	–
10	Compliance checking for adaptive business processes (Knuplesch et al. 2010; Ly et al. 2008a, b, 2010, 2012)	Independent of specific modelling language (implementation for ADEPT)	x	(Control flow conditions based on data properties)	–	–	x	–

(continued)

Table 4.2 (continued)

No.	Approach	Modeling language generalizability	Compliance rule generalizability			Evaluation		
			Simple	Medium complexity	Complex	Absence of evaluation	Against research gap	Against real-world
11	Compliance templates (Schleicher et al. 2010)	BPMN, BPEL	x	–	–	–	x	–
12	Compliance fragments and patterns; feedback based on CRT technique (Arbab et al. 2009; Elgammal et al. 2010; Kokash and Arbab 2009; Schumm et al. 2010)	BPMN, (BPEL, UML), each require an individual transformation to Reo models	x	(Data, temporal aspects)	–	–	(Implementation of prototype, demonstration using constructed scenario)	–
13	Verification of cloud-based workflows (Accorsi et al. 2011)	Petri Nets (transformation from BPMN possible)	(x)	(Data security aspects)	–	–	(Implementation of prototype and performance test)	–
14	Alignment of business processes and object lifecycles (Kuester et al. 2007)	UML activity diagrams	x	–	–	–	(Implementation of prototype and application to a framework)	–
15	Visual definition of resource compliance rules and verification (Wolter and Meinel 2010; Wolter et al. 2009)	BPMN	(x)	x	(Limited specification of organizational structure)	–	(Implementation of prototype, performance testing)	–

(continued)

Table 4.2 (continued)

No.	Approach	Modeling language generalizability	Compliance rule generalizability			Evaluation		
			Simple	Medium complexity	Complex	Absence of evaluation	Against research gap	Against real-world
16	PENELOPE (Goedertier and Vanthienen 2006)	BPMN	x	(Only activity operator can be defined)	–	x	–	–
17	Compliance pattern (Mueller 2010)	BPMN	x	–	–	–	(Implementation of prototype, performance testing)	(Demonstration using real-world scenario)
18	Tool support for verifying UML activity diagrams (Eshuis and Wieringa 2004);	UML activity diagrams	x	(Linear process flow + forks)	–	–	x	–
19	Symbolic model checking of UML activity diagrams (Eshuis 2006)	Process, data and organizational models	x	x	–	–	(Use of third-party tool)	–
20	Constraint-centric workflow change analytics (Wang and Zhao 2011)	All types of process models	x	(Data)	–	–	x	–
21	Automatic verification of data-centric business processes (Damaggio et al. 2011)	BPEL, Petri Nets	x	x	–	–	x	–

(continued)

Table 4.2 (continued)

No.	Approach	Modeling language generalizability	Compliance rule generalizability			Evaluation		
			Simple	Medium complexity	Complex	Absence of evaluation	Against research gap	Against real-world
22	How to implement a theory of correctness in the area of business processes and services (Lohmann and Wolf 2010)	BPEL, Petri Nets	x	x	–	–	(Use of third-party tool)	–
23	Transforming BPEL to Petri Nets (Hinz et al. 2005)	Extended BPEL	x	(Organizational units)	–	–	(Use of third-party tool)	–
24	Verifying BPEL workflows under authorisation constraints (Xiangpeng et al. 2006)	Extended UML activity diagrams	x	(Linear process flow + forks)	–	x	–	–
25	Pattern-based modeling and formalizing of business process quality constraints (Khaluf et al. 2011)	Petri Net dialect	x	(Data)	(Parallel execution)	–	(Use of third-party tool)	–
26	Data-flow anti-patterns: discovering data-flow errors in workflows (Trčka et al. 2009)	All types of process models	x	–	–	x	–	–

Adapted from Becker et al. (2012a)

Fig. 4.4 Generic
specification environment for
conceptual modeling
languages and models
(Becker et al. 2011a)

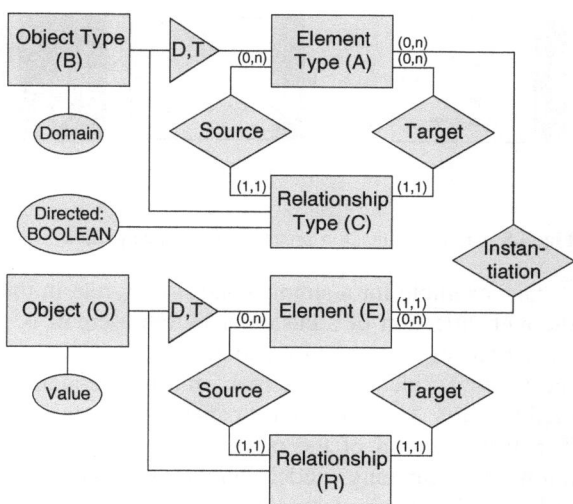

$G = (V, E)$ with $E \subseteq V \times V$. The basis of each model pattern builds a generic
specification of conceptual modeling languages, which comprises element types as
atomic model elements, object types, such as vertices, and relationship types, such
as edges. Particular model elements are instantiated from their element type and are
specialized in concrete objects and relationships. Figure 4.4 depicts the relationship
of model elements, objects, and relationship types as well as their instantiation.

The compliance checking approach uses set operations in order to define
compliance patterns that allow for a generic application regardless of the modeling
technique that was used for developing the process models. Altogether four categories of set operations for the pattern definition are supported by the approach
and its prototypal implementation (Becker et al. 2011a):

- Operations regarding specific properties of model elements (e.g., type, value, or
  domain).
- Operations that combine elements and relationships.
- Operations to build patterns representing a recursive structure.
- Operations that allow for a convenient and simplified pattern definition (oper-
  ations that are derived from those already introduced).

In order to demonstrate the general applicability of the approach, a proprietary
domain modeling language for business processes, the so called Semantic Business
Process Modeling Language (SBPML) (Becker et al. 2009), was applied to model
a credit application process. In addition, three types of compliance patterns are
defined: control flow rules, which comprise rules for the order of process activities,
resource rules, which contain all patterns about resources (e.g., IT-System or
agent), and business object related rules, such as special business object requirements (e.g., credit applications with a credit worth more than 75,000 EUR need
additional positive votes).

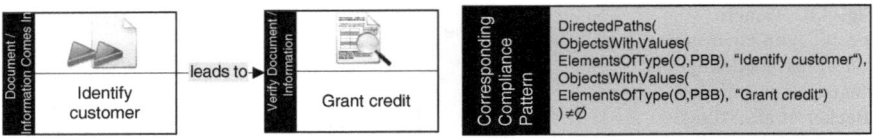

Fig. 4.5 Credit application process compliance pattern

One example for a simple control flow rule in the credit application process is the authentication of a customer before a credit is granted. In order to explicate such a rule as a compliance pattern, two activities need to be conceptualized. First, the activity "identify customer" must be conducted before the activity "grant credit" starts. The compliance pattern and its formalization is depicted in Fig. 4.5. The formalization of the pattern uses the set function "DirectedPaths", which allows for searching model elements that are linked to each other in a certain order. As input parameter, the function gets objects with values. In the example, these objects are model elements of the type process building block (PBB) containing the labels "identify customer" and "grant credit". If both activities appear in the process model, the function provides the set of elements and relationships of the whole path between the two activities. If the function returns an empty set, a compliance manager knows in this scenario that the process at hand is most probably not compliant because the pattern was not found.

4.2.3 Evaluation Method for Business Process Compliance Analysis Approaches

One essential result of the literature search (Becker et al. 2012a) is the obvious lack of practical evaluation for business process compliance analysis approaches. So far, only Mueller (2010) applied his approach in an industry setting. Nevertheless, Mueller (2010) did not explicitly evaluate the acceptance and relevance of compliance checking approaches, which motivates an evaluation of model-based compliance checking approaches for practical usage. Before such an evaluation can take place, an evaluation concept needs to be developed.

The evaluation concept for the compliance checking approach, developed and introduced in this book, makes use of the Technology Acceptance Model (TAM) (Davis et al. 1989; Venkatesh and Bala 2008), which is a theoretical framework for evaluating the usefulness and acceptance of IS. Since TAM is mainly introduced for quantitative studies, it is only applicable for a relatively large number of system users. However, it is unlikely that a financial institute would implement a prototype into its operational system landscape. Thus, a large quantitative study is not realizable at this early development stage.

According to Rosemann and Vessey (2008), the evaluation of IS artifact relevance can be performed even before the approach is company-wide implemented.

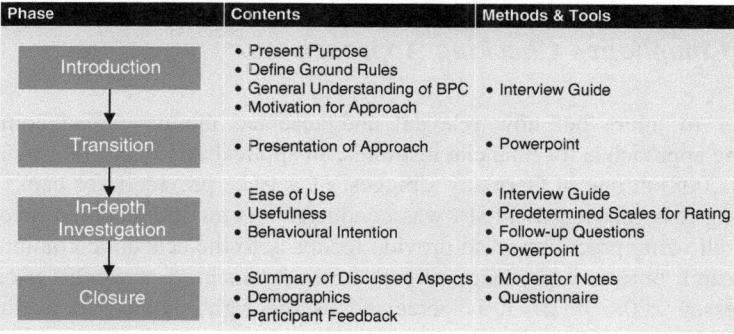

Phase	Contents	Methods & Tools
Introduction	• Present Purpose • Define Ground Rules • General Understanding of BPC • Motivation for Approach	• Interview Guide
Transition	• Presentation of Approach	• Powerpoint
In-depth Investigation	• Ease of Use • Usefulness • Behavioural Intention	• Interview Guide • Predetermined Scales for Rating • Follow-up Questions • Powerpoint
Closure	• Summary of Discussed Aspects • Demographics • Participant Feedback	• Moderator Notes • Questionnaire

Fig. 4.6 Evaluation procedure (Becker et al. 2012e)

The evaluation approach at hand is based on the focus group method (Gibson and Arnott 2007; Tremblay et al. 2010; Becker et al. 2012e). It comprises the TAM constructs job relevance, output quality, and perception of external control.

Job relevance is operationalized by the factors regulatory environment and process landscape. While regulatory environment describes the regulatory pressure of a company to comply with regulations, the factor process landscape describes the size and scope of the business process repository. The more business processes exist, the more effort is needed to check them for compliance issues. The output quality describes the extent to which user's result expectations are fulfilled. External control is operationalized by Business Process Management (BPM) maturity and BPM capability. BPM maturity is understood as the level of how advanced an organization is in applying BPM (Rosemann and de Bruin 2005). A high level of BPM maturity is perceived as a driver for business process compliance analyses. Additionally, BPM compatibility, i.e. the capability to integrate compliance analysis into the existing process model landscape, is also an important driver for the acceptance of such approaches. The other TAM constructs are rather irrelevant in that early step of evaluation because they cannot be rated subjectively without a constant usage of the system. In order to consider these special requirements and challenges, a focus group session-based concept is developed.

The evaluation procedure comprises four steps. In a first step, the topic and purpose of the evaluation workshop is presented. After this first step, the general functionality of business process compliance analyses is clarified and the interview approach is discussed. The transition phase contains the presentation of the compliance checking approach. The third step is the most extensive part and contains the investigation of the ease of use and usefulness of the approach as well as an in depth discussion about the behavioral intention to apply the approach in daily business situations. The final step is the closure phase, which mainly aims to validate the results and to check whether all information and discussion topics have been grasped properly. The whole procedure and the applied methods and tools are depicted in Fig. 4.6.

4.2.4 Relevance and Acceptance of the Developed Compliance Checking Approach

In order to figure out how relevant and accepted the developed compliance checking approach is for financial institutes, an applicability check (Rosemann and Vessey 2008) at one of Germany's biggest IT service providers for banks (In the following it is referred as ITSP) was conducted. As an applicability check is "a way of allowing practitioners to provide feedback to the academic community on the research objects it produces or uses in theory-focused research" (Rosemann and Vessey 2008, p. 2), it is perceived as the right method to evaluate the developed artifact. Therefore, the developed evaluation concept is applied.

From July until December 2011, a business process modeling and compliance project was conducted at ITSP, which has about 1,800 employees and serves around 450 banks. In order to serve the banks with a proper core banking system, all business processes must comply with internal and external regulations. The project had two goals. First, the sales and advice processes should be checked regarding their compliance. Second, a sufficient process description, including all related regulations and core banking modules, should be developed. Since the organization did not use any process management tools and modeling techniques at the beginning of the project, it was decided to use SBPML (Weiß and Winkelmann 2011) as modeling technique and the meta modeling tool [em] (Delfmann et al. 2008) to model and analyze the processes.

As a first step, relevant compliance rules for the sales and advice processes in a bank have been identified. These compliance requirements can be classified into four categories. The first category comprises *infringement patterns*, which identify missing process steps that are legally required. One example for such kind of patterns is the identification of sales and advice processes in which no consultation protocol is handed out to the customer, which is directed by law.

An example for a search result of an infringement pattern is depicted in Fig. 4.7. The corresponding pattern for a directed path between two process building blocks in a process model can be defined as follows (adapted from Becker et al. 2011a):

```
DirectedPaths(
    ObjectsWithValues(
        ElementsOfType(O,PBB),"Execute 2nd credit decision"
    ),
    ObjectsWithValues(
        ElementsOfType(O,PBB),"Create credit offer"
    )
)≠∅
```

The pattern searches for all process paths that contain building blocks containing the description "Execute 2nd credit decision" and "Create credit offer". Only when a second credit decision is executed, the credit offer is allowed to be created. The search algorithm shows all process paths in which these two activities

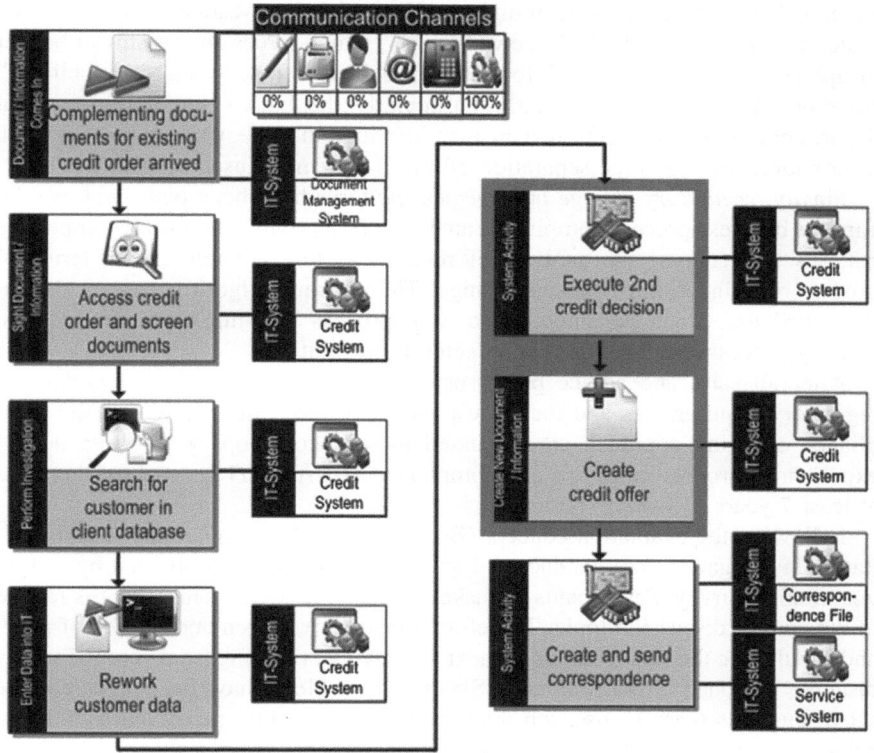

Fig. 4.7 Identified pattern in business process model

appear next to each other. In the small example in Fig. 4.7 two building blocks are identified by the pattern and the corresponding path is marked by a gray border.

The second pattern category contains *legal requirement identification patterns*, which identify process steps in which certain legal requirements need to be considered. In comparison to infringement patterns, patterns in this category identify process elements that are affected by regulatory requirements. An example for a legal requirement identification pattern is the search for all process building blocks of the type "Make Accounting Transaction" and "Make or Receive Payment". This analysis pattern supports compliance experts in identifying process elements that might be affected by the money laundry law.

The third pattern group comprises *risk management patterns*, which identify risks that influence a secure and compliant process execution. One law does not direct one particular risk pattern. Rather the identification and management of risks is an essential part of banking procedures (German banking law § 25a). One example for a risk management pattern is the usage of different IT systems in one path of a process. When different IT systems are used within the same process, the risk of inconsistent data storage or the occurrence of reentering data mistakes appears. In addition, the usage of different IT systems in investment processes may indicate a violation of the Chinese wall policy, which forces an investment banker to uphold "confidentiality of information provided to him by his firm's clients" (Brewer and Nash 1989, p. 206). Particularly the bank's internal investment department should not get such insider information. One way to prevent such information sharing is the separation of all IT systems in use.

Finally, *regulatory change management patterns* have been perceived as relevant for business process compliance analysis. This group contains all compliance patterns that support the analysis of regulations that are relevant in terms of process reengineering or process change. The matching algorithm uses a regulatory attribute, which is annotated to each process building block, in order to identify process elements that are affected by regulations.

After all sales and advice processes are modeled and checked regarding its regulatory requirements and the corresponding patterns, the results and the compliance checking approach are discussed in two workshops with altogether 14 experienced process managers and compliance experts of ITSP, each of them has at least 7 years of work experience.

Following the evaluation concept (Becker et al. 2012e), quantitative and qualitative investigations are conducted. Each qualitative part is motivated by a short quantitative survey. Participants are asked to evaluate one statement that is related to the current discussion topic. Therefore, they receive a pen and a piece of paper and should rate the statement that is next to the scale, reaching from zero ("I totally disagree") to one ("I totally agree"). Six discussion blocks have been prepared. The six discussions (ease of use, job relevance, output quality, perceived usefulness, behavioral intention, and frequency of usage) draw the same positive picture as it was explicated quantitatively by rating the statements. In the following, the discussion results are summarized with respect to the six discussion blocks.

Regarding the *ease of use* of the developed compliance checking approach, workshop participants stated that the application of the approach is of minor complexity when a general process orientation is established within ITSP. In 2011, ITSP had no formalized business processes, which is perceived as the major challenge for the implementation of a business process compliance management system. The development of business process models for analysis purposes would hinder the implementation of a process compliance analysis system. In addition, it was stated that the definition of patterns must be done in a way that any compliance violation can be detected.

The *job relevance* of the compliance checking approach is depending on the implementation of the approach into internal business processes. Participants discussed the need for a single regulatory influence process across department borders, in which the compliance checking approach is integrated. Focus group one discussed four tasks that can be supported by the compliance checking approach: usage during process modeling, usage for certifying of business processes, usage for the development of a compliance checking service as well as the usage for process maintenance and process change management.

The workshop participants described the *output quality*, i.e., the quality of the search results with respect to the completeness of the results, as "perfect". One essential prerequisite for this positive rating is the existence of an appropriate process model repository. Participants said that the quality of the results heavily depends on the quality of the process models. However, one improvement suggestion came up and was discussed. The participants were interested in a tabular listing of pattern search results, which is aligned to the role of the user. In this way, participants think to simplify the clarity of the pattern matching results.

The *perceived usefulness* of the demonstrated compliance checking approach was rated with medians of 0.63 and 0.66 (on a scale reaching from zero, indicating disagree to one, indicating agreement). One discussed advantage of the approach is the ability to show the customers of ITSP (in this case the customers are the banks) that the liability to ensure compliance was considered properly. Four major benefits of the approach for the daily work were discussed: Participants expect a workload reduction, the capability to identify process elements that are affected by regulatory changes, the usage for marketing purposes as well as the ability to identify regulatory affected core banking modules.

The discussion about the *behavioral intention* to use the demonstrated compliance checking approach reflects the quantitative ratings. Participants of both workshops agreed that they would use the approach under the condition that the business process models exist already. Both workshop groups said they would use the approach as a central means to check the regulatory compliance of business processes at ITSP. This positive feedback is also reflected by the rating of the *frequency of usage*, whose medians are 1.0 for the first focus group and 0.89 for the second focus group (on a scale from zero, indicating a very seldom usage frequency to one, indicating a very frequent usage). Participants would most certainly use the approach and only for some spot tests, they would check the business processes manually.

4.3 Reporting Compliance

Banks and insurance companies are directed to continuously submit reports about their current financial situation. Supervisory agencies require various information regarding the full range of activities and risk-management procedures (BaFin 2011), about the adequacy of capital according to regulations like Basel or its transformation into European law (EU CRD) (Bongaerts and Charlier 2009) as well as credit information (in particular large exposures) (Barron and Staten 2003; Cowan and de Gregorio 2003; Tsai et al. 2011). This dynamic national and international body of regulations steadily increases the effort to develop and maintain IS to fulfill these requirements. To address this increasing effort, the research work at hand aims to improve the conceptual modeling and analysis of regulatory reporting requirements for the design of IS (RQ3).

Therefore, the relevance and challenges of regulatory requirements for conceptual modeling needs to be identified in order to address RQ3.1. Based on these insights and for addressing RQ3.2, a modeling technique is developed to enable the conceptual specification of configurative reference models for regulatory reporting requirements (Eggert et al. 2013a). The modeling technique is evaluated and its effectiveness and efficiency in terms of designing data warehouses is determined. The developed modeling technique is implemented in a modeling tool in order to allow for analysing the developed conceptual models. The modeling tool, which supports the modeling and analysis of regulatory reporting requirements (Becker et al. 2012d), addresses RQ3.3. Finally, the modeling tool is applied in three modeling projects in order to address the last aspect of RQ3 and to provide insights into the applicability of the modeling technique for the conceptual modeling of regulatory reporting requirements (Becker et al. 2012b).

4.3.1 Challenges of Regulatory Reporting Requirements for Conceptual Modeling

Before a modeling technique and the corresponding modeling tool can be developed, it is meaningful to elicit the need for such a legal modeling approach. In order to determine the relevance of and challenges for regulatory requirements engineering, a multi-method approach, comprising the application of two focus group sessions (Stewart et al. 2007) and a structured literature review (vom Brocke et al. 2009; Webster and Watson 2002), was applied. The most important industry-related challenges of regulatory-driven requirements engineering are the basis for the analysis criteria of the literature review.

Participants of the focus groups were accounting and data warehouse experts. They work for an IT service provider for banks and different financial institutes as well as governing bodies. All participants worked on IS for the preparation of regulatory required reports and have several years of experience in designing such data warehouse (DW) systems and corresponding conceptual models.

Altogether nine topics regarding the conceptual modeling of regulatory requirements have been discussed during the workshops. The topics were evaluated quantitatively and qualitatively. For the quantitative part, a questionnaire was developed, in which one statement regarding each discussion topic should be rated. The nine statements and their ratings are depicted in Fig. 4.8.

Several challenges were discussed in the two workshops of which the three most important ones (the statements with the highest median in the quantitative survey are one, three, and seven) are described in the following. While discussing the feasibility of the navigation structure for regulatory requirements, it turned out that conceptual specifications are expressed textually and in an inhomogeneous structure. Requirement specifications of regulatory reporting obligations do not follow a clear guideline and thus contain different structures depending on the

No.	Statement	I totally agree	Result	I totally disagree	
1.	The navigation structure of the requirement specification enables an accurate identification of relevant details.	0	0,4 0,5 0,64	1	MIN: 0,18 MAX: 0,89
2.	Regulatory-driven requirement specifications are consistently designed.	0	0,32 0,37 0,61	1	MIN: 0,11 MAX: 0,72
3.	Avoiding double work during the requirement specification will be omitted systematically.	0	0,36 0,42 0,60	1	MIN: 0,09 MAX: 0,7
4.	Regulatory-driven report elements will be uniquely defined across all report definitions.	0	0,22 0,35 0,60	1	MIN: 0,15 MAX: 0,92
5.	All elements, that are affected by regulatory report requirement changes, can be identified easily.	0	0,27 0,39 0,59	1	MIN: 0,21 MAX: 0,66
6.	The requirement specification of regulatory-driven report requirements is totally compliant.	0	0,3 0,36 0,59	1	MIN: 0,16 MAX: 0,85
7.	The relationship between regulatory-driven report requirements and their technical transformation is traceable.	0	0,36 0,48 0,53	1	MIN: 0,08 MAX: 0,59
8.	The consistency between the IT implementation and the requirement specification will be supported ideally.	0	0,27 0,33 0,4	1	MIN: 0,06 MAX: 0,47
9.	Our requirement specification of regulatory-driven reports provides an optimal communication means for IT and business experts.	0 0,11 0,2 0,27		1	MIN: 0,07 MAX: 0,37

$n = 16$

Legend			
1. Quantil Median 3. Quantil		MIN Minimal value	
		MAX Maximal value	

Fig. 4.8   Rated statements from workshop participants

individual project. Thus, the search for requirement details and corresponding data warehouse elements is sophisticated. Participants state that they have to scroll through the whole requirements specification document in order to find a certain report. Furthermore, table rows and columns of reports are described textually and without a unique link to the corresponding data warehouse constructs, such as dimensions and ratios.

Another challenge is the avoidance of double work during the requirements specification process (statement three). All participants agreed that double work is caused by the lack of structure and the appearance of ambiguities in conceptual DW elements. One particular problem occurs when conceptual specifications stem from different departments, such as accounting and supervisory reporting. Participants agreed that the use of a centralized documentation of requirements for all stakeholders would be beneficial in order to prevent double work in the future.

The traceability between legal requirements and technical transformation (statement 7) was also perceived as a challenge for regulatory-driven requirements engineering. The goal of this discussion topic is to figure out how the identification of regulatory affected data warehouse constructs is conducted. To analyze the influence of regulations is important because it is an essential step in order to identify necessary changes in the data warehouse design. Again, the participants said that they use raw text search functions in order to retrieve affected tables and columns. "Currently, the identification of effects [of regulatory changes] for operational data is not simple", a member from the portfolio management of the IT service provider said. Now, there exists no linkage between regulations and data warehouse constructs or other technical implementations.

The literature review receives the most important challenges as input for analysing the literature review results. The rule for considering the challenge comprises two requirements. First, the mean value of the statement rating must be above 0.35. Second, the 3rd Quartile must be above the threshold of 0.5. In total, the statements 1–7 (cp. Fig. 4.8) have been regarded as analysis criteria in the literature review. The review was developed based on the search query: (regulat* OR law OR legal or norm) AND "requirements engineering" AND "Information system*". The query was applied on the scientific databases Ebscohost and Sciencedirect and revealed 495 articles, of which 26 are reviewed and 21 are relevant for regulatory-driven requirements engineering. Table 4.3 summarizes the classified results.

In particular three research gaps can be derived based on the focus group session and literature review results. First, a modeling technique is needed that supports the navigation and traceability of regulatory requirements. Second, a modeling tool is needed that allows for analysing conceptual requirements with respect to the impact of regulations. Third, the collaboration of IS experts and legal experts in regulatory-driven requirements engineering projects needs to be investigated from a behavioral perspective.

4.3.2 Development of a Modeling Technique for Regulatory Reporting Requirements

The challenges of specifying regulatory-driven requirements in interdisciplinary teams consisting of legal and IT experts are addressed by the development of a modeling technique for the development of configurative reference models. The solution approach follows three research goals (Eggert et al. 2013a). First, the modeling technique must be capable of developing conceptual models of regulatory reporting requirements. Second, the modeling technique needs to be used for the development of configurative reference models (Becker et al. 2007c; Fettke and Loos 2007b). Third, using the modeling technique must increase the effectiveness and efficiency of conceptual data warehouse design. For the development and evaluation of a suitable modeling technique, three research steps were conducted: the identification of relevant modeling technique elements, the development of a metamodel, and the evaluation of the developed artifact.

In order to identify required modeling technique elements for the development of regulatory required reports and the related data warehouse, the modeling technique constructs of established approaches (Gabriel and Gluchowski 1998) act as a basis for the analysis. Furthermore, language elements for the design of report requirements of the conceptual modeling technique H2 for Reporting (Fleischer 2013) have been analyzed. The relevance of the modeling language elements are

Table 4.3 Approaches addressing regulatory-driven requirements engineering

Result No.	Aiello and Lazovik (2006) 1	Antón et al. (2003) 2	Apostolou et al. (2011) 3	Bajec and Krisper (2005) 4	Breaux et al. (2009) 5	Crook et al. (2003) 6	Fernández-Medina et al. (2006) 7	Goossenaerts et al. (2009) 8	He and Antón (2009) 9	Ingolfo et al. (2013) 10
Industry-driven challenges of regulatory requirements engineering										
Support for navigation structure in requirement specifications										
Support for (consistent) requirement specification	x	x	x			x	x		x	x
Support for a systematical double work prevention			x	x	x			x	x	
Support for unique requirement definition	x	x					x		x	x
Support for tracing regulatory requirements	x		x		x					
Support for compliance checking of regulatory requirements	x	x			x				x	x
Support for tracing the technical impact of regulatory requirement changes				x				x		
Research paradigm										
Behavioral science oriented										
Design science oriented	x	x	x	x	x	x	x	x	x	x
Type of information										
Business process and functional perspective	x	x	x	x	x	x	x	x	x	x

(continued)

Table 4.3 (continued)

	Aiello and Lazovik (2006)	Antón et al. (2003)	Apostolou et al. (2011)	Bajec and Krisper (2005)	Breaux et al. (2009)	Crook et al. (2003)	Fernández-Medina et al. (2006)	Goossenaerts et al. (2009)	He and Antón (2009)	Ingolfo et al. (2013)
Result No.	1	2	3	4	5	6	7	8	9	10
Data perspective		x		x		x	x	x		
Type of investigated requirements										
Business rules	x			x						
Privacy and data access requirements		x				x	x		x	x
Regulatory/legal requirements			x		x			x		x

	Julisch et al. (2011)	Kardasis and Loucopoulos (2004)	Kartseva et al. (2005)	Liu et al. (2001)	Massacci et al. (2005)	Massacci et al. (2007)	Mouratidis et al. (2013)	Raus et al. (2009)	Rosca and Wild (2002)	Wan-Kadir and Loucopoulos (2004)	Weigand et al. (2011)
Result No.	11	12	13	14	15	16	17	18	19	20	21
Industry-driven challenges of regulatory requirements engineering											
Support for navigation structure in requirement specifications											
Support for (consistent) requirement specification	x		x	x	x	x	x		x	x	x
Support for a systematical double work prevention	x									x	

(continued)

Table 4.3 (continued)

	Julisch et al. (2011)	Kardasis and Loucopoulos (2004)	Kartseva et al. (2005)	Liu et al. (2001)	Massacci et al. (2005)	Massacci et al. (2007)	Mouratidis et al. (2013)	Raus et al. (2009)	Rosca and Wild (2002)	Wan-Kadir and Loucopoulos (2004)	Weigand et al. (2011)
Result No.	11	12	13	14	15	16	17	18	19	20	21
Support for unique requirement definition		x									
Support for tracing regulatory requirements										x	
Support for compliance checking of regulatory requirements	x		x	x		x			x		
Support for tracing the technical impact of regulatory requirement changes											
Research paradigm											
Behavioral science oriented								x			
Design science oriented	x	x	x	x	x	x	x		x	x	x
Type of information											
Business process and functional perspective	x	x	(x)	x	x	x	x		x	x	x
Data perspective	x	x			x	x	x			x	
Type of investigated requirements											
Business rules	x	x	(x)		x	x	x		x	x	x
Privacy and data access requirements											
Regulatory/legal requirements	x			x				x		x	(x)

indicated by analyzing four different laws for supervisory reporting of banks, namely the Solvency and Liquidity Act, the MiFID, and equity requirements from Basel III. Table 4.4 depicts the legal text excerpts that require the corresponding modeling technique elements. In addition, the first column contains the name of the corresponding construct in different modeling languages.

Legal requirements can be classified using their deontic function (for deontic logic, see von Wright (1951) and Risto (2001)). In order to enhance the clarity of regulatory elements, they are classified as *obligation*, *prohibition*, *exemption*, or as *permission*. In addition, elements to define links to specific legal concepts (*qualification*) or to allocate competencies to executive institutions (*power*) (for this visualization approach, see Mahler (2010)) are used.

Another requirement for a suitable modeling technique is derived from regulatory constraints regarding the reporting differences among different types of financial institutes. Several regulatory requirements are allocated to a special group of financial institutions, such as home loan banks or securities trading banks. Section 269 of the German Solvency Act, for example, states that "financial service institutes trading financial instruments on their own account as well as securities trading banks may alternatively use special methods for determining the administrative cost-based capital requirement approaches to the capital charge for operational risk." In order to represent such requirements comprehensively for a larger group of stakeholders, the conceptual DW model needs to be configurable.

The identified requirements for a regulatory-driven DW modeling technique are used for an extension of the modeling technique H2 for Reporting. Figure 4.9 depicts the basic constructs of H2 for Reporting (grey shaded boxes) and its extension to represent regulatory reporting requirements. In particular, the regulation element was added and connects the basic DW and report elements (dimension, ratio, dimension scope, report, layout, cube, and filter) via a ternary relationship and a validity attribute, which may explicate validity constraints, such as the validity period of a law. The regulation element allows for annotating regulatory requirements to a conceptual DW model element for expressing and classifying the source of the regulatory requirement. A regulation may reference to other regulations and can be distinguished into deontic and non-deontic functions. External regulations represent the legal requirements from the law directly. They might be very generic in many cases. Internal regulations are company-individual specializations or interpretations of external regulations. They express that an external regulation was interpreted and specialized by an internal business rule or guideline.

Based on this meta-model, a configuration extension was added to the modeling language in order to allow for configuring models depending on the individual application scenario (Fig. 4.10). The grey shaded boxes in Fig. 4.10 indicate the constructs from the meta-model depicted in Fig. 4.9. Therefore, a report element is connected with a configuration term, which expresses the configuration rule for the model configuration. It is associated with configuration parameters and corresponding values. In this way, it can be expressed that, for example, a certain report

Table 4.4 Identified regulatory reporting requirements

Concept	Solvency act	Liquidity act	MiFID	Basel III
Dimension/Hierarchy ME/RM: Dimension ADAPT: Dimension/ Hierarchy DFM: Hierarchy XBRL: Dimension	§ 55, paragraph 2, sentence 1: "The IRBA positions according to § 71 are assigned to IRBA debt claim classes according to §§ 73 to 83." Thus, an IRBA debt claim class consists of n IRBA positions	§ 3 and § 4 define the hierarchical structures of liquid assets and liabilities, respectively. These structures are also demonstrated by reporting forms LV 1 and LV 2 in Annexes 2 and 3	§ 4, no. 1(3) states that, "ancillary service' means any of the services lists in Section B of Annex I", while Annex I categorizes several reference objects as investment services and activities, ancillary services, and financial instruments	§ 49: "[...] For each of the three categories above [...] there is a single set of criteria that instruments are required to meet before inclusion in the relevant category." Thus, instruments are subordinate to categories
Instance object ADAPT XBRL	In § 2, paragraph 3, sentence 2, market risk positions are listed: "[...] (1.) foreign currency positions [...], (2.) commodity positions [...], (3.) trading book positions [...], and (4.) other market risk positions [...]."	§ 3 and § 4 list a set of reference objects that influence the facts of liquid assets and liabilities, respectively (e.g., central banks, financial institutions, customers, securities, bills of exchange)	§ 4, paragraph 1, no. 2 defines investment services and activities as „services and activities [...] relating to any of the financial instruments [...]." Further, no. 26 defines branch as "a place of business other than the head office [...]".	§ 90: "The following items [...] will receive a 1250 % risk weight: certain securitisation exposures, certain equity exposures [...], non-payment/ delivery on [...] transactions, and significant investments in commercial entities."
Ratio ME/RM: Attribute ADAPT: Dimension Member DFM: Fact Attribute (Measure) XBRL: Primary Item	§ 307, paragraph 3, sentence 1, no. 3 directs the requirement for the definition of net income and debt ratios: "[...] assets and liabilities, net earnings and business operations [...]" have to be shown	§ 2, paragraph 1: "The liquidity [...] is considered to be sufficient if the [...] liquidity ratio is not less than the value one."	Annex II, I, no. 2, for example, categorizes clients to be professionals if any two of the following size requirements are met: balance sheet total of 20 million euros, net turnover of 40 million euros, own funds of 2 million euros	§ 40: "The LCR is intended to promote resilience to potential liquidity disruptions over a 30 day horizon." Further, § 51 generally defines the term "bank" as "bank, banking group or other entity [...] whose capital is being measured."

(continued)

Table 4.4 (continued)

Concept	Solvency act	Liquidity act	MiFID	Basel III
Ratio system ADAPT: measure dimension	In § 2, paragraph 2, the conditions for meeting the capital requirements are defined. A corresponding ratio system consists of the ratios total capital charge, capital charge for operational risk and available equity	§ 2, paragraph 1, sentence 2 defines how the liquidity ratio is calculated: the quotient of available liquid assets and liabilities during maturity band 1	§ 27 obligates investment firms to provide public firm quotes. Those quotes have to be calculated and, thus, depend on other ratios	§ 91 states that "banks which disclose ratios involving components of regulatory capital […] must accompany such disclosures with a comprehensive explanation of how these ratios are calculated."
Report XBRL	§ 335, paragraph 2: "[…] have to report the following information in quantitative terms: […] actual losses in form of direct depreciations and value adjustments in the previous reporting period for each asset class […]."	§ 11 requires that institutions have to disclose their ratios and defines how this is to be done.	§ 28, paragraph 1 requires that investment firms disclose "the volume and price of […] transactions and the time at which they were concluded."	§ 149 requires that banks "ensure that their countercyclical buffer requirements are calculated and publically disclosed […]."
Report layout XBRL	Report Form 2 in Appendix 3 requires that balance-sheet credit risk positions and offsetting positions […] have to be shown line-by-line and eligible financial guarantees column-by-column	Reporting forms LV 1 and LV 2 in Annexes 2 and 3 demonstrate a report layout of § 11: liquid assets and liabilities are listed in the rows; check sums, weighting factors, and the capital charges of maturity bands 1–4 set up the columns	MiFID does not provide concrete report layout requirements. Rather national laws (i.e. the German WpHMV) direct concrete report layouts	Annex 3 illustrates, for example, that assets as well as liabilities and equity of the parent bank and the subsidiary are listed row-wise by having the corresponding bank-specific facts in the columns

(continued)

Table 4.4 (continued)

Concept	Solvency act	Liquidity act	MiFID	Basel III
Report attribute XBRL	§ 6, paragraph 1, sentence 1: "Institutions have to submit reports [...] to the German federal bank." And in § 36, paragraph 2, no. 3: "For investment assets, a report will be prepared at least annually [...]."	§ 11 requires that the ratios have to be reported to the German Federal Bank. The report frequency is monthly or semi annually	§ 10, paragraph 5, sentence 2: "At least once a year, investment firms shall also inform the competent authority [...] of shareholders and members [...]." § 19, no. 8 requires that clients "must receive [...] adequate reports [...]."	§ 117 expands/replaces some Basel II requirements. For example, an update of § 49(i) requires that the risk control unit produces and analyzes daily reports.
Reference object attribute XBRL	The disclosure requirements for securitizations under § 334 require the institutes to disclose, for example, the name of the credit rating agency and the nature of securitized debt.	The report templates attached to the liquidity act (i. e. report template LV1) contain additional information like customer name, institute ID or the place of institute. These elements are conceptualized by reference object attributes	Article 10, paragraph 5, sentence 2: "investment firms shall also inform the competent authority of the names of shareholders and members [...]." § 25, no. 4: "The reports shall [...] include details of the names and numbers of the instruments [...]."	Section 105 defines a portfolio capital charge for Credit valuation adjustment. To be able to calculate that ratio each single name hedge must include ist rating and weight according to Table 105

Eggert et al. (2013a)

is solely obligatory for a home loan bank or that ratio calculations differ depending on the type of bank.

The modeling technique was evaluated in two laboratory modeling experiments with 25 IS master students, 22 of which participated in the first experiment and all 25 participated in the second experiment. The first experiment tests the ability to develop and configure a conceptual model using the developed modeling technique in comparison to the usage of the corresponding law text. The whole group of students was randomly divided into two groups. One group received the configurable H2 for Reporting model, the other group received the corresponding law text. Table 4.5 summarizes the results regarding the model correctness and the correlation with the group attendance. Table 4.6 provides the processing time (minimum, maximum, and mean) that is needed by each group (group A received the law text, group B received the model). Table 4.7 expresses the correlation between the processing time and the group attendance. The results indicate that using the developed modeling technique for regulatory requirements specification enables a faster model development process and results in qualitatively better conceptual models.

The second experiment tests the ability to develop a snowflake schema based on a model that was developed with the introduced modeling technique. The control group received the corresponding law with the same task. Table 4.8 summarizes the experiment results and classifies them with respect to the type of mistakes the respondents did. In addition, correlation results regarding the model correctness and the group attendance indicate a significant correlation between the model group attendance and the development of correct models. Table 4.9 provides the correlation results with respect to the processing time and group attendance and Table 4.10 provides the average processing time of the groups. The second modeling experiment draws the same picture like the first one. Both experiments confirm that by providing a configurative reference model the tasks were conducted significantly faster and provided significantly better model results in terms of modeling mistakes.

4.3.3 Modeling Tool for Regulatory Reporting Requirements

The metamodel of the extended modeling technique (cp. Figs. 4.9 and 4.10) is implemented into the hierarchical metamodeling tool H2-Toolset (Fleischer 2013) (Becker et al. 2012d). Two reasons lead to the decision to choose this modeling tool. First, as metamodeling tool, the H2-Toolset does not only support modeling with the basic version of H2 for Reporting. Rather it allows for extending the modeling technique by adding new language constructs. Thus, the basic version of the language H2 for Reporting, which was already implemented in the H2-Toolset, could be easily extended. Second, the plug-in architecture of the H2-Toolset allows for an easy extension of the modeling tool's functionalities. Import, export, analysis, transformation, and further information processing capabilities are examples

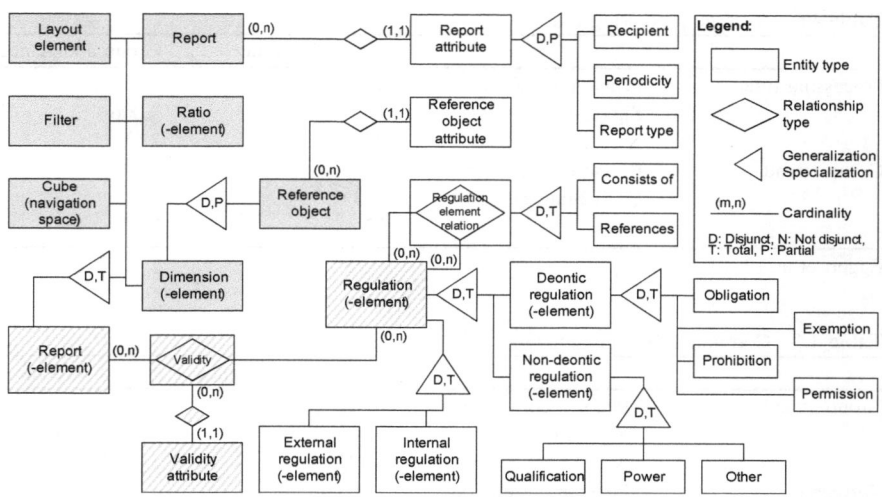

Fig. 4.9 H2 for reporting metamodel and extension for regulations (Eggert et al. 2013a)

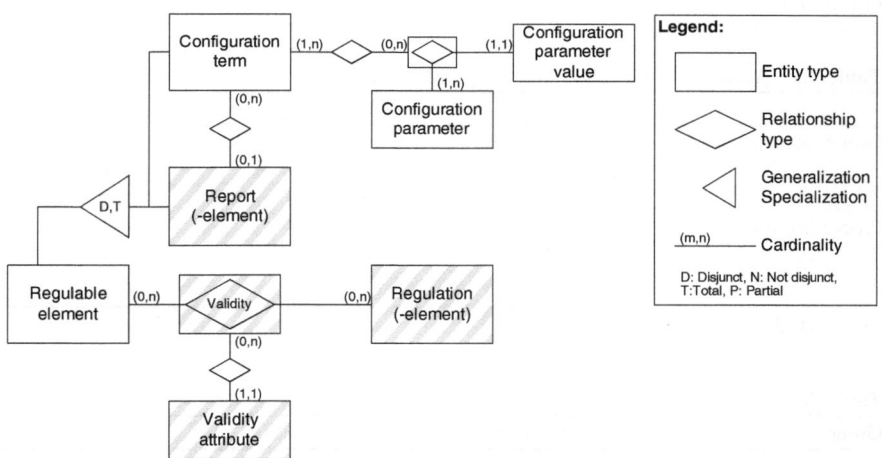

Fig. 4.10 Configuration extension of the H2 for reporting metamodel (Eggert et al. 2013a)

Table 4.5 Correlation between group attendance and model correctness

Group attendance	Mean (h)	N	Missing	Minimum (h)	Maximum (h)
A (text)	00:10:49	12	1	00:01:16	00:15:02
B (model)	00:06:33	10	2	00:03:40	00:09:46

See Eggert et al. (2013a)

Table 4.6   Average processing time

		Processing time	Group attendance
Processing time	Pearson correlation	1	−0.564
	Sig. (2-tailed)	–	0.006
	N	22	22
Group attendance	Pearson correlation	−0.564	1
	Sig. (2-tailed)	0.006	–
	N	22	22

Eggert et al. (2013a)

Table 4.7   Correlation between processing time and group attendance

		Group attendance	Correctness
Group attendance	Pearson correlation	1	−0.600
	Sig. (2-tailed)	–	0.003
	N	22	22
Correctness	Pearson correlation	−0.600	1
	Sig. (2-tailed)	0.003	–
	N	22	22

Eggert et al. (2013a)

Table 4.8   Accuracy of modeling in inquiry-task three

		Group attendance	Processing time
Group attendance	Pearson correlation	1	−0.637
	Sig. (2-tailed)	–	0.001
	N	25	25
Processing time	Pearson Correlation	−0.637	1
	Sig. (2-tailed)	0.001	–
	N	25	25

Eggert et al. (2013a) ·

Table 4.9   Correlation between group attendance and time

Group attendance	Mean (h)	N	Std. Deviation (h)
A (text)	00:12:15	13	00:02:17
B (model)	00:08:57	12	00:01:50
Total	00:10:40	25	00:02:38

Eggert et al. (2013a)

for such functionality extensions. In particular the analysis of regulatory influenced model elements can be realized by using the model analysis plug-in of the H2-Toolset (Becker et al. 2012d).

The conceptual data structure of the H2-Toolset is depicted in Fig. 4.11. The basic idea of the H2-Toolset is the summary of all model element types in so-called contexts. A context contains the model element types, for example,

Table 4.10 Average time effort and group attendance

Group attendance (Correctly modeled?)		Frequency	Percent	Valid percent	Cumulative percent
A (text)	No, wrong/missing dimension levels	6	46.2	46.2	46.2
	No, multiple reasons	7	53.8	53.8	100.0
	Total	13	100.0	100.0	
B (model)	Yes	10	83.3	83.3	83.3
	No, wrong order	2	16.7	16.7	100.0
	Total	12	100.0	100.0	–

Eggert et al. (2013a)

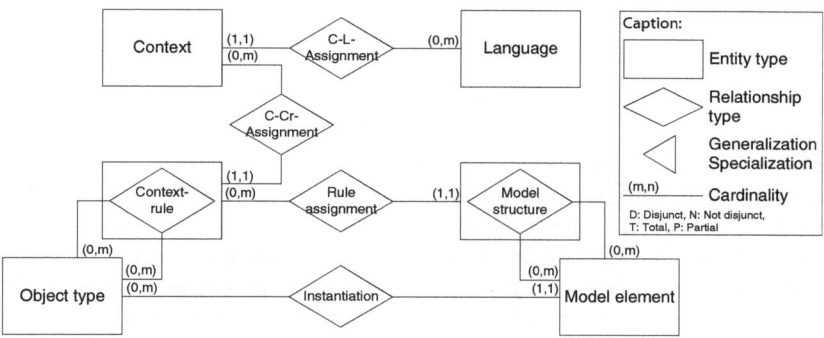

Fig. 4.11 Conceptual data structure of the H2-toolset. Adapted from Becker et al. (2012d)

dimensions, ratios, and reports, which can be used in a concrete multidimensional DW and report model. The relationship between the concrete objects of a context, for example, the dimensions and ratio objects, can be defined by using context rules. They express the grammar of the modeling technique. Finally, the developed model appears as a set of model elements that are combined in a model structure.

The identified challenges for regulatory reporting compliance (cp. Fig. 4.8) indicate the need for an analysis function for conceptual report and DW models (Statement 1, 5, and 7). In order to trace regulatory influences on reports and report elements, two analysis types are required (Becker et al. 2012d):

- Analysis from a legal perspective (Type 1). A dynamic legislative, such as the regulatory body for financial institutes, leads to a steady change of regulations. The compliance of supervisory reports needs to be ensured at any time. Thus, supporting the tracing of regulatory effects on DW model elements is a central requirement for a suitable model analysis approach.

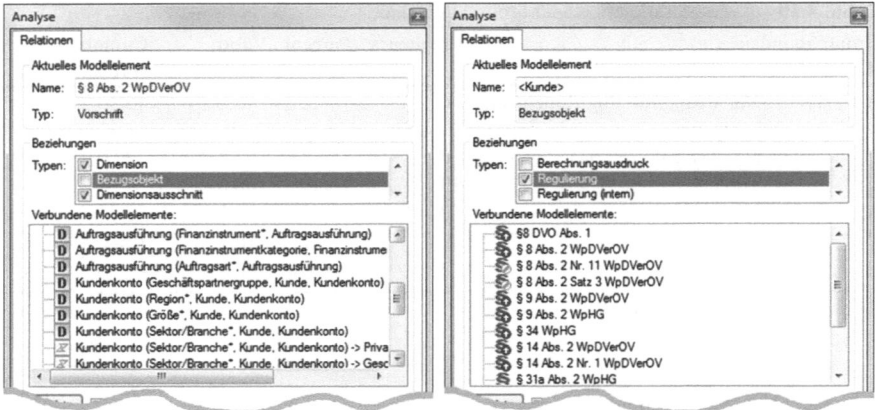

Fig. 4.12 Analysis from a legal (Type 1) and report perspective (Type 2) (Becker et al. 2012d)

- Analysis from a report perspective (Type 2). From a report perspective, an analysis to track affected regulations in terms of report changes must be enabled. When reports in a financial institution change, for instance because of a changed ratio calculation, the affected regulations must be identified in order to conduct a compliance check. Thus, another model analysis requirement is to trace the regulatory elements that are allocated to a report or report element.

The developed modeling technique allows for adding regulatory requirements to model elements, which is one central prerequisite for analysing regulatory influences on reports and DW elements. After implementing the modeling technique into the H2-Toolset, a sample report model regarding an excerpt of the European MiFID and its German implementation has been developed. Figure 4.12 exemplarily depicts the analysis functionality of the H2-Toolset. In the left part of the figure, the analysis of all dimensions and dimension scopes that are affected by § 8 Section 2 of the German Investment Services Conduct of Business and Organization Regulation are listed (analysis type 1). On the right side, all regulatory elements that belong to the dimension customer are listed (analysis type 2).

4.3.4 Application

In three extensive modeling experiments, the developed modeling technique and its tool implementation were applied for developing conceptual DW and report models of regulatory reporting requirements for financial institutions (Becker et al. 2012b). Three regulations have been modeled: The German Large Exposure Act, reporting requirements according to Basel III, and the German Liquidity Act. Besides addressing RQ3.4, the goals of these modeling projects are 2 fold. First,

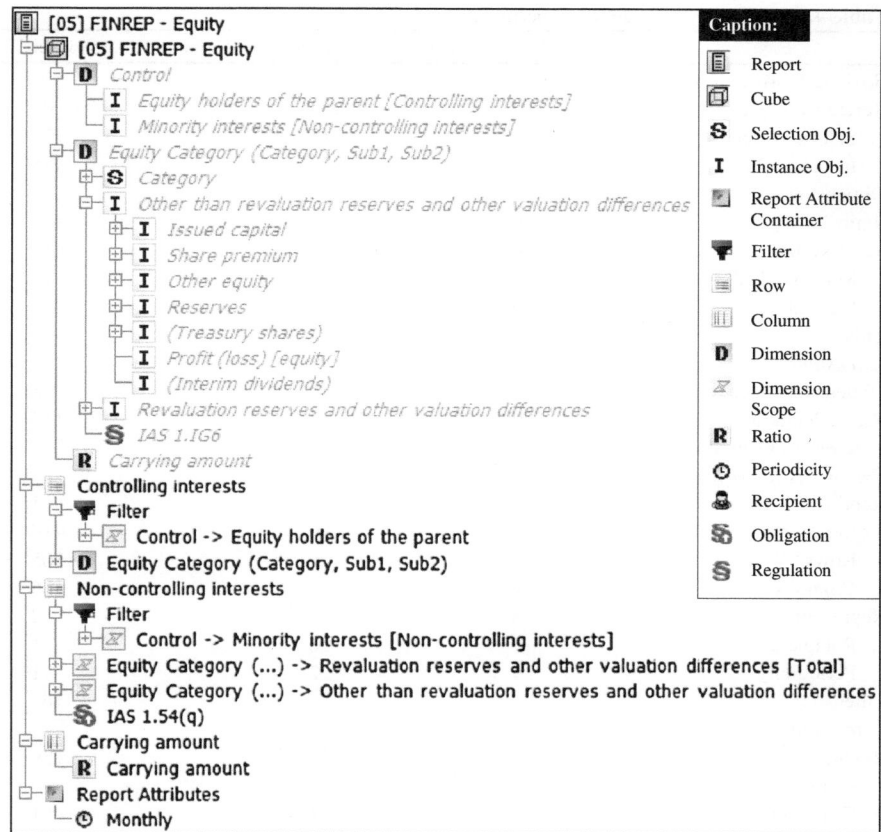

Fig. 4.13 Basel III equity report model excerpt (Becker et al. 2012b)

evidence for the applicability of the developed modeling technique should be provided. Second, insights into the challenges and best practices for the modeling of regulatory requirements should be received.

All modeling experiments took place in 2011. For the Large Exposure Act as well as for the Basel III equity requirements, two groups of five IS Bachelor students participated in the corresponding modeling projects. The Liquidity Act is much smaller and needs less effort for modeling. Thus, only one student worked on this regulation. The modeling tool of choice was the H2-Toolset (Eggert et al. 2013a) and the implemented modeling technique was H2 for Reporting with its legal extension (cp. Figs. 4.9 and 4.10). Figure 4.13 depicts a sample model of a Basel III equity report. After the development of all regulatory required reports and report elements, the database, which stores all model information, was queried in order to receive the number of used model elements. The results are summarized in Table 4.11.

Table 4.11 Results of modeling experiments

	Liquidity act	Large exposure act	Basel III
Basic data warehouse concepts			
Reference object	139	152	1,107
Selection object	22	13	172
Instance object	117	139	935
Dimension	9	12	93
Ratio	16	69	117
Ratio system	6	21	11
Mathematical	6	14	10
Logical	0	7	1
Cube	1	13	46
Extensions			
Dimension scope	57	56	376
Fact calculation	80	59	117
Reference object attribute	0	0	6
Extensions for report representation			
Report	3	23	45
Report layout	19	0	410
Rows	15	0	305
Columns	4	0	105
Report attribute	18	50	2
Recipient	9	28	1
Periodicity	9	22	1
Filter	0	0	164
Extensions for regulation representation			
Regulation	191	538	739
Deontic			
Obligation	30	64	291
Exemption	16	14	17
Prohibition	0	14	14
Permission	2	30	23
Non-deontic			
Qualification	68	128	141
Power	0	10	0
Other	75	278	253
Regulation element relation	184	535	716
Consists of	153	129	716
References	31	406	0
Validity	164	294	881
Validity attribute	32	22	0

Adapted from Becker et al. (2012b)

Except the modeling language constructs Logical Ratio Systems, Power, and Reference Object Attribute, all modeling language elements were used frequently in order to develop the conceptual models for the analyzed regulations. The reasons for the low usage frequency of these three modeling language elements are

2 fold. Either these two constructs are no suitable modeling constructs for supervisory regulations or these two constructs are too complex to grasp for the participating students in the projects.

Altogether five lessons learned could be retrieved from the modeling experiments (Becker et al. 2012b). First, IS students need special courses about the understanding of regulatory and banking specific terms before they begin to model. It turned out that translating regulatory requirements into data structures is pretty challenging for IS students. Second, all participants had serious problems to identify data warehouse constructs. One solution for a better training procedure is the preparation of a repository for common regulatory expressions and to teach the allocation of expressions with conceptual data warehouse constructs. Third, the regulations contain requirements that the modeling technique cannot capture at the moment. Thus, the modeling technique has to be extended in order to handle requirements, such as threshold values for the liquidity ratio (cp. § two, section two, Liquidity Act). Fourth, a clear procedure for handling references to other laws needs to be defined at the beginning of the modeling project. Since not all referenced requirements can be part of the conceptual model because of clarity reasons, the qualification element should be used in order to represent a reference to other laws (e.g., for term definitions). Fifth, based on the experiences within the modeler teams, one should prepare a handbook for model granularity and follow a sentence-by-sentence modeling. One group modeled the regulatory requirements sentence by sentence, while the Basel III group used an undefined analysis procedure. The results indicate that this group had serious problems to identify the deontic function of a regulation. Thus, it is recommended to use a sentence-by-sentence approach (Becker et al. 2012b).

4.4 Collaboration of IS Experts and Legal Experts

The application of the developed approaches for business process and reporting compliance in financial institutes requires a collaboration of IS experts and legal experts. This section conceptualizes the perceived relationship of IS and legal experts from both a practice and research perspective and provides means to support the collaboration (RQ4). From a practical perspective, the collaboration of IS and legal experts in regulatory-driven IT projects is investigated (RQ4.1). From a research perspective, the perceived relationship of IS and law is investigated by analyzing relevant IS research papers (RQ4.2). Finally, the third aspect of RQ4 is addressed by means of developing a solution to exchange, classify, and analyze the interdisciplinary research artifacts from information law and legal informatics (RQ4.3).

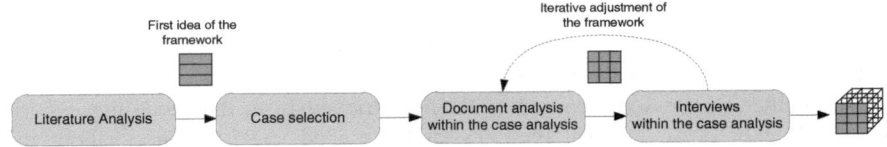

Fig. 4.14 Framework development process (Knackstedt et al. 2012)

4.4.1 Relationship of IS and Law from a Practical Perspective

In order to investigate the perceived relationship of IS and law in regulatory-driven IT projects, the German online car registration project, is investigated. The goal of this research work is to develop a classification framework that might be used to classify perceptions of IS and legal experts in regulatory-driven IT projects. For the framework development an iterative research approach, consisting of the steps literature analysis, case selection, document analysis, and the conduction of interviews was chosen (see Fig. 4.14).

Five criteria led to the selection of the online car registration case. First, the interaction between IS and legal actors is essential for the success of the project at hand. Second, the chosen project combines system planning activities and the consideration of legal requirements. Third, since the German online car registration project is a typical IT project, in which IT and legal experts need to work together, the generalizability of the case results is assumed. Fourth, an in-depth investigation of the project's details is possible due to the availability of interview partners. Fifth, the investigation of the selected project does not lead to considerable ethical problems, such as disadvantages for interview partners.

The framework for the perceived influence of IS and law in regulatory-driven IT projects comprises three dimensions, namely the perceived influence direction, the perceived influence character, and the perceived influence impact (Fig. 4.15). The *perceived influence direction* can have three values. It distinguishes between the directions 'Law influences IS' (Law → IS), IS influences Law (IS → Law), and for situations, in which both IS and law influence each other the bi-direction link (Law ← → IS) is established. The dimension *perceived influence character* distinguishes between a positive, negative, and ambivalent character of a certain situation of the investigated project situation, depending on the perceived individual consequences of the project situation under investigation. The last dimension classifies the *perceived influence impact*. The perceived impact of regulatory requirements or technical developments can be classified as restrictive, demanding or enabling. A project situation will, for example, be classified as restricting when the law constraints possible functions of IS. A demanding situation appears when, for example, technological developments demand for a regulatory change or vice versa. One example for a perceived enabling situation is the development of new technological solutions, as an effect of the enactment of

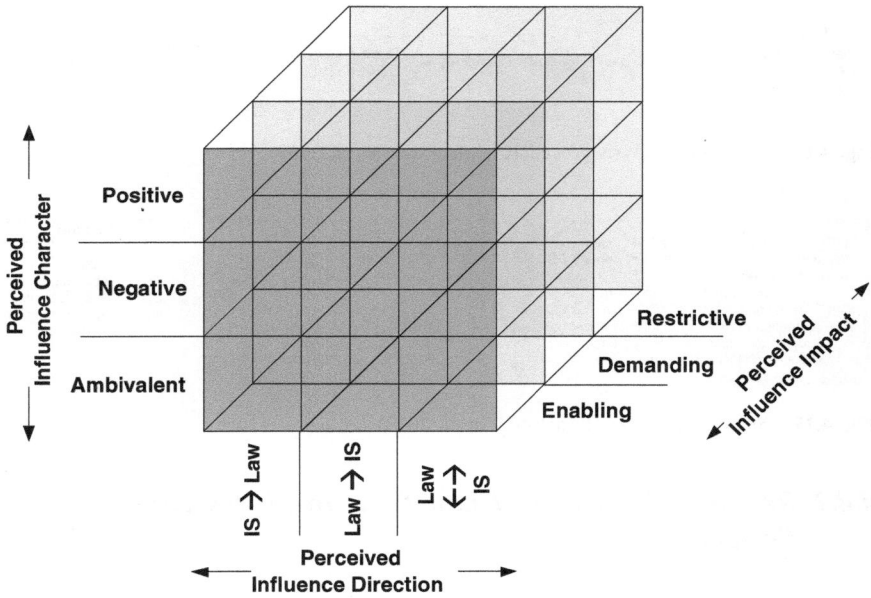

Fig. 4.15   Framework for the relationship of IS and law (Knackstedt et al. 2012)

paragraph 91 c of the German constitution. It allows the collaboration of the federal government, the federal states, and municipalities regarding the planning and provision of IT services (Knackstedt et al. 2012).

The whole framework is depicted in Fig. 4.15 and can be used in order to evaluate the perception of team members in regulatory-driven IT projects. Knowing these perception dimensions establishes an early awareness and helps project managers to control IT projects through the timely implementation of preventive measures. The analysis of the e-Government case led to four lessons learned for regulatory-driven IT projects (Knackstedt et al. 2012). First, IT projects need a committee for the collaborative identification of solutions. This committee must contain legal as well as IT experts. Second, means to establish a common ground are needed. In particular, modeling techniques are perceived as one solution to overcome the communication gap between legal and IT experts. Third, risks regarding the legal consequences of IT developments and the technological consequences of the law (and law changes) need to be communicated and a common understanding of them needs to be established. Fourth, goal ambiguities need to be considered from the planning of IS until the implementation. A goal ambiguity in terms of regulatory-driven IT projects exists, for example, when legal experts aim to keep the current situation because legal risks are already known and minimized in the current situation, while IT experts aim to improve the processes because it is technically feasible.

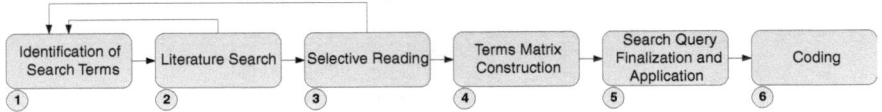

Fig. 4.16   Literature analysis procedure (Knackstedt et al. 2013)

(TI("information systems") OR AB("information systems") OR SU("information systems") OR KW("information systems") OR TI("information scien*") OR SU("information scien*") OR KW("information scien*") OR TI("legimatics") OR AB("legimatics") OR TI("computer science") OR AB("computer science") OR SU("computer science") OR KW("computer science"))	A N D	(TI("law*") OR AB("law*") OR SU("law*") OR KW("law*") OR TI("legal*") OR AB("legal*") OR SU("legal*") OR KW("legal*") OR TI("regulat*") OR AB("regulat*") OR SU("regulat*") OR KW("regulat*") OR TI("compliance") OR AB("compliance") OR SU("compliance") OR KW("compliance") OR TI("de jure") OR AB("de jure") OR SU("de jure") OR KW("de jure"))	**Caption**

			TI	Title,
			AB	Abstract,
			SU	Subject terms,
			KW	Author-Supplied Keywords

Fig. 4.17   Search parameter (Knackstedt et al. 2013)

4.4.2 Relationship of IS and Law from an IS Research Perspective

After the previous section outlined the perceived relationship of IS and law from a practical perspective, this section describes the interrelationship from a scientific perspective. Based on an extensive literature analysis the goal is to provide insights into the perceived relationship of IS and law from IS researchers' perspective. The research method to develop the results is based on a six-step procedure, comprising the identification of search terms, the literature search, a selective reading, the construction of a search term matrix, the search conduction, and the result coding (see Fig. 4.16). The applied search query parameter for the database query in Ebscohost and ScienceDirect is depicted in Fig. 4.17.

The literature review comprises 53 relevant articles. An article is perceived as relevant when it is about a regulatory topic or when the law plays a significant role in this article. For coding, the articles are read and separate statements are classified among the dimensions influence direction and influence impact (cp. Fig. 4.15). The third dimension (perceived influence character) was omitted due to missing data. Solely by reading an article, the perceived influence character of the authors cannot be retrieved. Instead the application domain is added to the coding schema. It classifies the main application domain of the investigated IS in the research articles, such as IS applied in the economic domain. The results of the coded statements are summarized in Table 4.12.

One example for a coded text section is a statement in the article by Chai et al. (2011): "As a result, we conclude that legislative efforts contribute to increasing awareness of the importance of information security and to arousing attention to information security investment announcements" (Chai et al. 2011, p. 659). This passage was rated as a perceived enabling influence of the law on IS. In Table 4.12 this passage appears as one statement in the dark grey shaded area. The results

Table 4.12 Results of the analysis (Absolute and relative text occurrences)

Direction and impact domain (IS)	IS → Law restricting	IS → Law demanding	IS → Law enabling	Law → IS restricting	Law → IS demanding	Law → IS enabling	Total
Economic domain	0	34 (14 %)	7 (2.9 %)	23 (9.5 %)	78 (32.1 %)	50 (20.6 %)	192 (79 %)
Legal domain	2 (0.8 %)	0	16 (6.6 %)	0	6 (2.5 %)	2 (0.8 %)	26 (10.7 %)
Governmental domain	0	2 (0.8 %)	6 (2.5 %)	2 (0.8 %)	12 (5 %)	3 (1.2 %)	25 (10.3 %)
Total	2 (0.8 %)	36 (14.8 %)	29 (11.9 %)	25 (10.3 %)	96 (39.5 %)	55 (22.6 %)	243 (100 %)

Knackstedt et al. (2013)

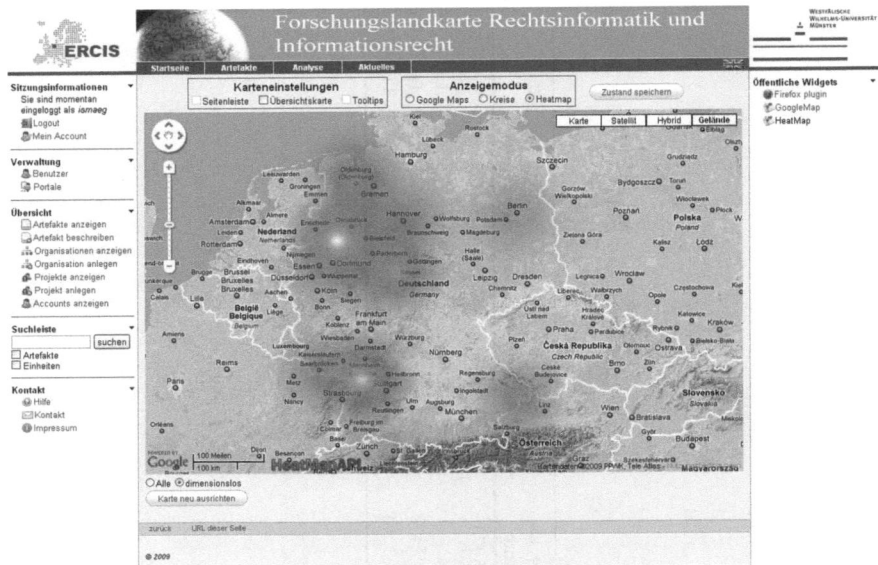

Fig. 4.18 Graphical analysis of research portal data (Excerpt)

provide evidence that the major perceived relationship of IS and law is characterized by a demanding position regarding regulations that influences IS in the economic domain.

4.4.3 Research Portal

For supporting the collaboration of IS and legal researchers (RQ4.3), a research portal for the interdisciplinary exchange of research results at the border of legal informatics and information law is developed (Knackstedt et al. 2010). The developed research portal provides five functionalities. First, users may publish summaries of research results. Second, the portal provides predefined classification criteria for research results, which prevents a heterogeneous and arbitrary research description. Third, the portal allows for searching research results in two ways: By using the classification criteria and by using a full text search. Fourth, analyses on the entered data are enabled. These (statistical) analyses allow for identifying research gaps. Figure 4.18 depicts an excerpt of the map-based analysis functionality and provides information about the density of distributed research output in the involved organizations (the brighter the shaded areas, the more research output is generated based on the portal data). Fifth, the scientific discourse is supported by a Wiki-concept and its change management capabilities.

Data of the research portal can be classified in organizations, projects, and research results. Research results in the area of legal informatics and information law can be classified by various dimensions. The research portal contains six important classification dimensions and predefined values:

- Application domain (industry independent, chemical industry, finance, health, interorganisational systems, public administration, etc.)
- Application focus (internal, B2B, B2C, etc.)
- Addressed profession (privacy law, information law, legal informatics, etc.)
- Practical usage (1–5, 6–10, more than 10, no practical usage so far, etc.)
- Degree of finalization (development finished, in development, etc.)
- Involved field of law (public law, penal law, civil law, etc.)

This classification and structuring of research results allow for a gap analysis in order to find research areas that were not addressed in the past. One search query could ask, for example, for all research results involving public law, practical application, and focusing on B2B application scenarios.

Chapter 5
Discussion and Outlook

5.1 Contributions to Research and Practice

Four research questions (RQ1–RQ4) drive the contributions of this book. Figure 5.1 provides an overview of the research areas, the developed solutions and research findings as well as the contributions to research (indicated by a black circle) and practice (indicated by a black diamond). In the following discussion, all contributions are referenced by the corresponding number (CR1–CR28 and CP1–CP14).

5.1.1 Identification of the Influence of Regulation on IS Design (RQ1)

Two aspects of research question RQ1 were addressed in this book. A quantitative study among 105 IT experts indicates that models and analysis methods have a significant impact on regulatory-driven IT projects. A significant relationship between the integration of compliance and legal experts in IT projects and the usage of formalization and analysis methods could be found. The research contribution of this study is 3 fold. First, an exploratory model was tested for the first time and offers insights into the influenced MIS organizational variables in a regulatory environment (CR1). Second, the results shed light on the extent to which MIS variables, such as executive commitment and user involvement, influence MIS success in a regulatory environment (CR2). Third, and most importantly for the work at hand, the study results motivate further research on model-based compliance management (CR3) and thereby addresses RQ1.1. Furthermore, the managerial implications of the study are 2 fold. First, it could be proven that MIS success increases when compliance experts are involved in regulatory-driven IT projects (CP1). Thus, a Chief Information Officer (CIO) should consider the involvement of legal and compliance experts in such regulatory-driven projects. Second, the study results indicate that the usage of formalization and analysis methods may close communication gaps between legal and IS experts and increases MIS success (CP2).

M. Eggert, *Compliance Management in Financial Industries*,
SpringerBriefs in Information Systems, DOI: 10.1007/978-3-319-03913-8_5,
© The Author(s) 2014

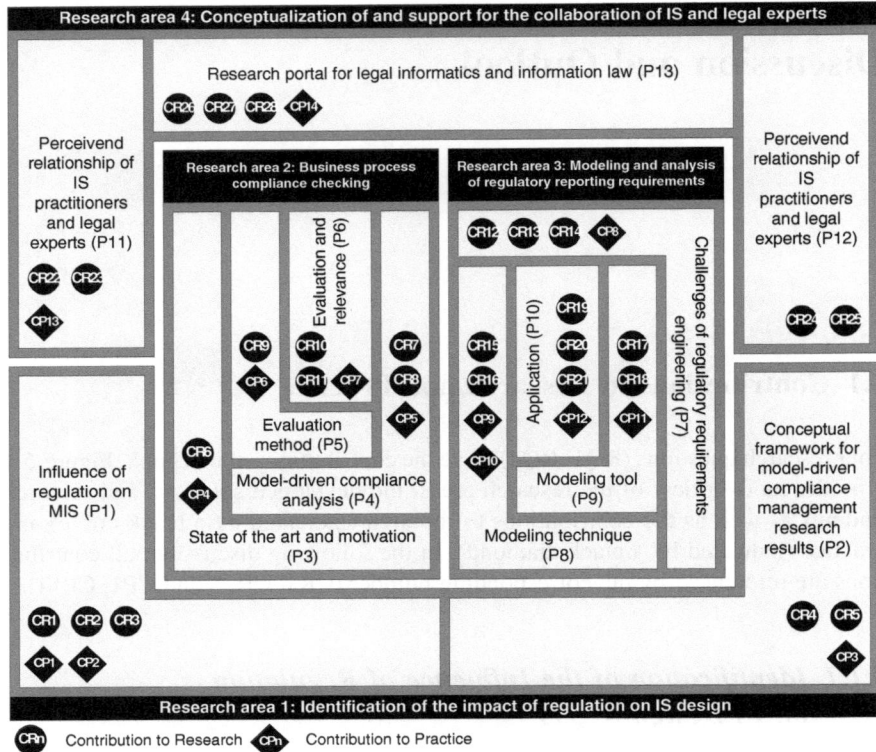

Fig. 5.1 Contributions to research and practice

Based on the relevance of conceptual modeling for regulatory-driven IT projects, a classification framework was developed in order to classify model-based compliance management research results. The framework contains three dimensions (domain, model level, and type of research) and addresses the second aspect of research question RQ1. Researchers can use these dimensions to classify research results of model-based compliance management (CR4). Furthermore, the framework can be used as a foundation for the development of a research roadmap in which novel research areas are depicted (CR5). Practitioners may use the classification framework for finding modeling and model analysis approaches as well as other research results about the applicability of such approaches in real-world scenarios (CP3).

5.1.2 Improving the Efficiency and Effectiveness of Business Process Compliance Checking (RQ2)

Five aspects of research question RQ2 were investigated in this research area. An extensive literature analysis was conducted in order to shed light on the current state of business process model analysis approaches. Altogether, 26 approaches were found and analyzed regarding their modeling language and compliance checking generalizability in order to address RQ2.1a. Based on these findings, further research potential was identified and a research roadmap was presented RQ2.1b. Thereby, the results contribute to the body of knowledge in several ways. From a research perspective, the literature search reveals two major research gaps. First, current compliance checking approaches are either not generally applicable in terms of models developed with different modeling techniques or they are not applicable with the whole body of compliance patterns. Second, the approaches lack a proper evaluation of their usefulness for the industry. Based on these research gaps, an agenda for further research work to develop and evaluate design-time compliance checking approaches was developed (CR6). From a practical perspective, the literature search provides a list of adoptable approaches, which might be applied in real-world projects. Compliance experts and CIOs are informed about approaches that may be tailored for their individual needs (CP4).

In order to address the identified research gap, an approach for checking various compliance rules in business processes, modeled with various modeling techniques, was developed. Through the semi-automatic analysis of business process models, the approach efficiently supports compliance assessments and thereby addresses RQ2.2. The developed prototype provides two research contributions. First, the applicability of the theoretically motivated approach could be demonstrated by using the developed metamodeling prototype. Business process models, developed with a proprietary building block-based modeling technique, were checked regarding several different compliance rules (CR7). Second, the approach and its prototypic implementation provide a basis for an applicability check and an extensive evaluation in a real-world scenario (CR8). From a practical perspective, the generalizability of the approach allows for using it in different industry environments, regardless of the applied modeling technique or compliance rules (CP5). Companies, in particular financial institutes, may use the approach in order to check their business process models for compliance frauds and regulatory requirements.

For the evaluation of the introduced business process compliance checking approach a suitable evaluation concept, based on focus group sessions, was developed and addresses RQ2.3. The approach combines quantitative research elements from TAM (Venkatesh and Bala 2008; Venkatesh and Davis 2000; Venkatesh et al. 2003) with qualitative elements of an applicability check (Rosemann and Vessey 2008). Therefore, the developed evaluation concept provides a generalizable and comparable way for evaluating business process compliance checking approaches. Researcher may use this evaluation concept in order to enhance the comparability of evaluation results of different compliance checking approaches (CR9). Industry may use this approach in order to check whether a certain business process compliance checking approach is suitable and whether internal prerequisites for using semi-automated business process compliance checking are given (CP6).

Finally, the evaluation method was empirically applied in a business process compliance project within one of Germany's biggest IT service providers for banks. The project comprises the modeling of both business process models and compliance rules. Furthermore, the models were checked regarding regulatory compliance by using the compliance rules modeled. In the end, two workshops have been conducted, following the question guideline and procedure of the developed evaluation approach in order to answer RQ2.4 and to shed light on the acceptance of a generalizable compliance checking approach for financial industries. The results provide evidence that the developed compliance checking approach is very useful when the business process model repository exists in such a way that it can be analyzed by a formal checking approach. The contributions for research are 2 fold. First, the relevance and acceptance of business process compliance checking approaches could be proven in a real world setting (CR10). IS researchers receive insights into the applicability of a compliance analysis approach. Second, concrete compliance patterns are provided in order to repeat the checking experiments in other environments and with other approaches (CR11). Practitioners get insights into thoughts of compliance and business process experts regarding the usefulness and application requirements of business process compliance checking approaches (CP7).

5.1.3 Improving the Effectiveness and Efficiency of Conceptualizing Regulatory Reporting Requirements (RQ3)

Besides the analysis of business processes, this book also contributes to the investigation of approaches for regulatory compliant report and DW design (RQ3.1). Therefore, an industry study and literature review was conducted in order to derive challenges of regulatory-driven data warehouse requirements engineering processes. The challenges and shortcomings in current regulatory-driven DW development processes were identified in two focus group sessions with banking and DW experts and by conducting a literature review. Among others, a missing traceability of effects of regulatory changes on the DW, a lack of navigation structure of requirement specifications, and non-consistent requirement documentations were revealed. Additionally, redundant work during the specification of regulatory requirements was strongly discussed by workshop participants. Based on these discussions, a literature review was conducted in order to identify research gaps. Based on the results, a research agenda was developed for further research regarding the requirements engineering process for regulatory-driven IT projects. This work's contribution to research is 3 fold. First, it provides insights into requirements engineering processes of banks and their IT service providers. It thoroughly describes the challenges for IT and legal experts when they need to work in an interdisciplinary team and sheds light on the reflection in scholarly literature (CR12). Second, the identified challenges motivate a deeper investigation of the interaction between IS and legal experts in regulatory-driven IT projects (CR13). Third, researchers may use the research agenda for developing new artifacts for supporting the requirements engineering process of regulatory-driven data warehouse projects (CR14). Practitioners from financial industries may use the discussion results and challenges for a better preparation and awareness for challenges in their own regulatory-driven DW projects (CP8).

The identified challenges led to the development of a model-based solution. To represent and trace regulatory requirements in conceptual DW and report models, a modeling technique was developed that can be used for developing configurative reference models of regulatory-driven DW requirements. The developed modeling technique was evaluated by conducting laboratory modeling experiments, whose results indicate that using reference models will increase the efficiency and effectiveness of the conceptual design of DWs in a regulatory environment. Thereby, the second aspect of research question three (RQ3.2) was addressed. This work provides two research contributions. First, a conceptual modeling technique for regulatory report requirements is presented and tested with financial supervisory report requirements from different regulations (CR15). Second, the extent, to which the efficiency and the effectiveness of using the modeling technique are accelerated and improved, was determined (CR16). The experimental results can be used for conducting further studies and for comparing these results with the experimental results at hand. Practitioners benefit from this work in two ways. First, IT and legal experts receive a modeling technique, which is applicable to the conceptual design of regulatory reporting requirements (CP9). The technique can be used for own DW projects in order to increase the efficiency and effectiveness of the conceptual design phase. Second, supervisory agencies, such as the European Central Bank and the German Federal Bank, may use the modeling technique in order to develop conceptual reference models for DW requirements in addition to the legal texts in the law (CP10).

In order to apply the developed modeling technique, a modeling tool is necessary that allows for developing and analysing conceptual models for regulatory report requirements. The third aspect of the research question RQ3 was addressed by the implementation of the developed modeling language into the meta-modeling tool H2-Toolset. In a sample application, the analysis capabilities of the modeling tool could be used for tracing the effects of regulatory changes on DW constructs and vice versa. The successful implementation of the modeling technique provides two essential research contributions. First, the applicability of the developed modeling technique could be demonstrated by the use of the prototypal implementation (CR17). Second, the modeling tool can be applied in further modeling experiments in order to evaluate the usefulness and feasibility of the developed modeling technique (CR18). From a practical perspective the modeling tool can be used in DW projects to build-up a well-structured model repository, which can be analyzed regarding the impact of regulatory changes (CP11). In this way, the developed artifact addresses the challenges, identified in the workshops (see Sect. 4.3).

As a final step for answering research question RQ3, the developed conceptual modeling technique was evaluated regarding its capability to represent regulatory reporting requirements. RQ3.4 was addressed by conducting three extensive modeling experiments with IS bachelor and master students. The results provide evidence that the majority of the modeling technique elements are (mostly) necessary and applicable for the requirements engineering process of legal supervisory reporting obligations. The work provides three contributions for research and practice. First, the applicability of the developed modeling technique was investigated for three supervisory-related regulations (CR19). Second, the modeling projects provide lessons learned for further regulatory-driven modeling projects, which are relevant for both research and practice (CR20 and CP12). Third, based on the combination of legal visualization and IS, the research results motivate a discussion about an interdisciplinary perspective of information modeling and legal visualization (CR21).

5.1.4 Conceptualizing and Supporting the Collaboration of IS and Legal Experts (RQ4)

Model-based compliance management is strongly coupled with the collaboration of IS and legal experts in regulatory-driven IT projects. In order to provide insights into the collaboration of IS and legal experts from a practical perspective, a case study about a regulatory-driven IT project was conducted and addresses RQ4.1. A framework was developed for the classification of the perceived relationship of IS and legal experts in regulatory-driven IT projects. The framework consists of three dimensions (influence character, influence direction, influence impact), with which the relationship of IS and law in such IT projects can be described. The work's contribution to research is 2 fold. For the first time the collaboration of IS and legal experts was investigated and the perceived relationship between these two stakeholder groups were conceptualized in a multidimensional framework (CR22). Researchers may use the developed framework for comparing the behavior of IT and legal experts in different regulatory-driven IT projects. In addition, the framework may build a basis for a structured literature review about the relationship of IS and law in scholarly publications (CR23). From a practical perspective, the framework can be used to support the management of regulatory-driven IT projects and to learn from the experiences, described in the case study (Knackstedt et al. 2010). When project managers are aware of the different perceptions of stakeholder in regulatory IT projects, the solution finding process and implementation of preventive measures is supported.

Besides the investigation of the perception of IS and law in IT projects, this book also provides insights into the perceived relationship of IS and law in a part of the IS research community. The goal to investigate how IS researchers perceive and reflect the relationship of IS and law (RQ4.2) was reached by conducting an extensive literature review in top IS journals and conference proceedings. The results provide evidence that the developed classification framework, containing the dimensions influence character and influence direction, can be applied for describing the perceived relationship of IS and law in IS research. The work contributes to research in two ways. First, IS researchers receive a classified overview about the perceived relationship of IS and law in IS outlets (CR24). Second, based on these findings, the results provide implications for an interdisciplinary research perspective on IS and law in future IS research (CR25).

Research at the border of IS and law is mostly published in different outlets. Thus, researcher groups that work on closely related topics need much effort to find each other and to collaborate. The third aspect of research question RQ4.3 addresses this problem and demands for a solution to classify and analyze research artifacts from IS research and law. The solution contains the development of a web-based research portal, in which research organizations can publish structured descriptions of their research results and corresponding research projects. In this way, the portal collects interdisciplinary literature and contributes to a combined perspective on regulatory-driven IS topics (CR26). The developed artifacts and study results in this book, for instance, can be classified among the portal dimensions. Thus, legal academics can get access to the results and possibly takeover or extend some ideas. In addition, researchers can use the portal to identify research gaps (CR27). Furthermore, researchers as well as practitioners may use the portal in order to receive an overview about research organizations that work on legal informatics, information law, and IS related topics (CR28 and CP14).

5.2   Limitations

The results presented in this book have limitations, which are covered in the corresponding research papers to some extent. Five further limitations exist that cover the book as a whole.

First, this book comprises 13 autonomous publications and manuscripts, which have been published in or submitted to different outlets. The final version of each publication is the result of the consideration of several different reviewer comments and improvement suggestions. Due to different calls for papers or publication invitations, each publication was written for a certain application context. Therefore, the communicated findings of this work vary among the different articles, for example, regarding their style, depth of details, and terminology.

Second, this work perceives model-based compliance management from an IS perspective. Results from other disciplines, such as legal visualization, were not primarily investigated and compared with the artifacts at hand. In addition, besides the contingency theory (Galbraith 1973; Lawrence and Lorsch 1967), other theoretical foundations for investigating and explaining the influence of regulations on the organization of IT departments may be used.

Third, the developed business process and reporting compliance approaches were mainly applied at one financial institute. To generalize the results, further applications in other organizations of financial industries are necessary. Furthermore, the problem of inconsistent terms in process modeling was not addressed by the presented approach. Even if a building block based modeling technique, such as the SBPML for banks (Becker et al. 2010b), decreases the likelihood of name conflicts, it might be possible that process element names in the business process model and in the compliance pattern diverge. In this case, the pattern would not match to the business process model and the analysis will most likely return no results. First attempts for semantic standardization of information models and the prevention of term conflicts have been presented by Delfmann et al. (2009) and Thomas and Fellmann (2009). Furthermore, the majority of patterns that have been described in this book are valid for only a small number of business processes. The efficiency advantages of semi-automated business process compliance analysis are raised when the compliance checking approach assesses several business process models. Thus, compliance patterns that can be applied across business process and department borders need to be investigated in the future.

Fourth, the development of a modeling technique for regulatory reporting requirements presumes that the financial institution is responsible for the development and maintenance of the reporting systems. If core-banking software was bought by a software supplier or the bank is not in charge of software maintenance, this firm will not belong to the main target group of the developed modeling technique. Furthermore, the modeling technique was developed based on several regulation text excerpts. Nevertheless, its completeness in terms of all legal reporting requirements remains unclear. So far, the developed modeling technique was not applied in a real industry project, which prevents a statement regarding the general acceptance of the modeling technique. In particular, the usefulness of reference models has only been argued and tested in a laboratory experiment. Experiences in real DW development projects need to be investigated in further research works.

Fifth, the collaboration of IS and legal experts was not investigated in a project that applies the artifacts introduced in this book. It was not investigated how the perceived relationship of IS and law changes or how it is influenced when compliance checking and conceptual modeling and analysis techniques for regulatory requirements are applied.

5.3 Outlook

The findings of this research work comprise several new insights into compliance management in financial industries and the collaboration of IT and legal experts in general. Based on the research work at hand, a couple of further questions need to

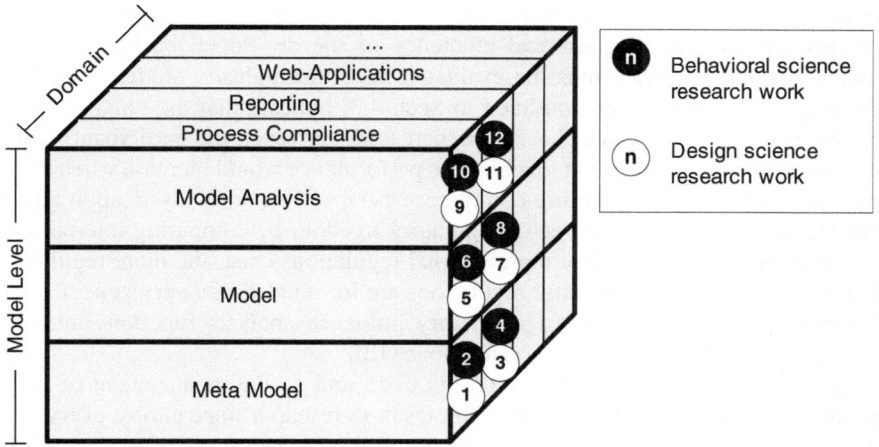

Fig. 5.2   Research outlook classification. Adapted from Becker et al. (2012c)

be answered in the future. The classification framework, introduced in Sect. 4.1, is applied to classify further behavioral science and design science research work (Fig. 5.2). In the following, the research topic addressed is referenced by the corresponding number in the classification framework (1–12).

At the metamodel level, four research topics need to be investigated in further research work. First, a process modeling technique that fulfills the specific requirements of legal experts needs to be developed (1). Approaches for process modeling techniques that include regulatory requirements exist (e.g., Alpar and Olbrich 2005), but their applicability was not proven so far. In particular, legal experts may have other requirements for a suitable business process modeling technique then IS experts. A new or extended modeling technique for regulatory requirements must be evaluated among legal experts as well as IT experts in order to prove its feasibility (2). For reporting compliance, the developed and extended modeling technique H2 for Reporting must be evaluated in a real world project (4). Based on the findings and specific requirements from legal experts, the modeling technique needs to be justified (3).

The model level comprises the development of configurative reference models for regulatory-influenced business processes and reports (5 and 7). In order to develop configurative reference models, the developed modeling technique for regulatory reporting requirements can be applied. In addition, the reference models must be evaluated in real regulatory IT projects. Particularly, the acceptance and applicability of the reference models by legal experts should be part of further investigations (6 and 8).

Finally, new artifacts need to be developed in order to increase analysis capabilities for report and business process models. So far, the definition of compliance patterns is only feasible by using a formal mathematical approach. In further research work the development of an interface for a graphical representation and reuse of compliance patterns should be developed (9). From a behavioral science perspective, the effectiveness and efficiency of the developed business process model analysis approach must be evaluated in further industry studies (10). The focus group session results, outlined in Sect. 4.3, indicate that the efficiency and effectiveness of compliance checks are increased. However, the participants could not determine the exact extent to which the performance would increase when using the approach. From a reporting compliance perspective, an analysis approach is needed to determine the degree of regulatory freedom by comparing internal and external regulations (11). The more internal regulations exist, the more regulatory freedom a company has because regulations are formulated in a very general way. Furthermore, the usefulness of regulatory influence analysis functions must be evaluated in further empirical investigations (12).

The regulatory influence on the design of IS and on the management of organizations is one of the most upcoming topics in IS research since almost every new enacted regulation has a significant influence on IS. In the past, requirements for IS mainly stem from departments and business units within the borders of organizations. Nowadays, more and more requirements originate from a dynamic and volatile regulatory environment and legislature, particularly in financial industries. The dynamic legislature indicates that the trend towards an increasing regulatory body will not end in the near future. Rather, it is expected that the effort to design regulatory compliant information systems and business processes, in particular in financial industries, will increase steadily. This book provides a few solutions and guidelines to tackle these challenges and to build up an effective and efficient compliance management.

References

Abdullah, N., Indulska, M., & Sadiq, S. (2009). A study of compliance management in information systems research. *17th European Conference on Information Systems*. Verona, Italy

Abdullah, S. N., Sadiq, S., & Indulska, M. (2010). *Emerging challenges in information systems research for regulatory compliance management*. Hammamet: CAISE.

Abelló, A., Samos, J., & Saltor, F. (2006). Yam2: A multidimensional conceptual model extending Uml. *Information Systems Research, 31*(6), 541–567.

Acharya, V. V., & Richardson, M. (2009). Causes of the financial crises. *Critical Review: A Journal of Politics and Society, 21*(2–3), 195–210.

Aguilar-Savén, R. S. (2004). Business process modelling: Review and framework. *International Journal of Production Economics, 90*(2), 129–149.

Aiello, M., & Lazovik, A. (2006). Monitoring assertion-based business processes. *International Journal of Cooperative Information Systems, 15*(3), 359–389.

Alberti, M., Chesani, F., Gavanelli, M., Lamma, E., Mello, P., Montali, M., & Torroni, P. (2007). Expressing and verifying business contracts with abductive logic. In G. Boella, L. van der Torre & H. Verhagen (Eds.), *Normative multi-agent systems* (dagstuhl seminar no. 07122). Dagstuhl, Germany: Internationales Begegnungs- und Forschungszentrum fuer Informatik.

Alpar, P., & Olbrich, S. (2005). Legal requirements and modelling of processes in e-Government. *The Electronic Journal of e-Government, 3*(3), 107–116.

Alves, A., Arkin, A., Askary, S., Barreto, C., Bloch, B., & Curbera, F. (2007). *Web services business process execution Language V2.0*. Organization for the Advancement of Structured Information Standards (OASIS).

Antón, A. I., Earpb, J. B., & Carter, R. A. (2003). Precluding incongruous behavior by aligning software requirements with security and privacy policies. *Information and Software Technology, 45*, 967–977.

Apostolou, D., Mentzas, G., Stojanovic, L., Thoenssen, B., & Pariente Lobo, T. (2011). A collaborative decision framework for managing changes in e-Government services. *Government Information Quarterly, 28*, 101–116.

Archer, L. B. (1984). Systematic method for designers. In N. Cross (Ed.), *Developments in design methodology* (pp. 57–82). London, UK: John Wiley.

Awad, A. (2010). *A compliance management framework for business process models*. Potsdam: University of Potsdam.

Baacke, L., Fitterer, R., Rohner, P., & Stroh, F. (2010). *Using semantically annotated models for pattern-based process analysis*. Switzerland, St. Gallen: University of St. Gallen

BaFin. (2011). Minimum requirements for risk management (Mindestanforderungen an Das Risikomanagement) Marisk. Retrieved November 24, 2011 from http://www.bundesbank.de/download/bankenaufsicht/pdf/marisk/071030_rs.en.pdf.

Bajec, M., & Krisper, M. (2005). A methodology and tool support for managing business rules in organisations. *Information Systems, 30*, 423–443.

Bandara, W., Gable, G. G., & Rosemann, M. (2005). Factors and measures of business process modelling: Model building through a multiple case study. *European Journal of Information Systems, 14*, 347–360.

Barron, J., & Staten, M. (2003). The value of comprehensive credit reports: Lessons from the U.S. experience. In M. Miller (Ed.), *Credit Reporting Systems and the International Economy*. Boston: MIT Press.

Barth, A., Datta, A., Mitchell, J., & Nissenbaum, H. (2006). Privacy and contextual integrity: Framework and applications. *2006 IEEE symposium on security and privacy* (pp. 184–198).

Barth, J. R., Caprio, G., & Levine, R. (2004). Bank regulation and supervision: What works best? *Journal of Financial Intermediation, 13*, 205–248.

Bashar, N., & Easterbrook, S. (2000). Requirements engineering: A roadmap. *22nd International Conference on Software Engineering (ICSE '00)* (pp. 35–46). Limerick, Ireland.

Batini, C., Ceri, S., & Navathe, B. (1992). *Conceptual database design—An entity-relationship approach*. Redwood City: Benjamin/Cummings.

Becker, A., Förschler, D., & Klein, J. (2007a). *Mifid: Umsetzungsanleitung Und Umsetzungsprüfung Für Die Praxis Von Banken Und Sparkassen*. Frankfurt am Main.

Becker, J., Algermissen, L., Pfeiffer, D., & Räckers, M. (2007). Bausteinbasierte modellierung von Prozesslandschaften mit der picture-methode am Beispiel Der Universitätsverwaltung Münster. *Wirtschaftsinformatik, 49*(4), 267–279.

Becker, J., Bergener, P., Delfmann, P., Eggert, M., & Weiss, B. (2011a). Supporting business process compliance in financial institutions—A model-driven approach. *Internationale Tagung Wirtschaftsinformatik (WI2011)*, Zurich, Switzerland.

Becker, J., Breuker, D., Weiss, B., & Winkelmann, A. (2010a). Exploring the status quo of business process modelling languages in the banking sector—An empirical insight into the usage of methods in banks. *21st Australasian Conference on Information Systems*, Brisbane, Australia.

Becker, J., Delfmann, P., Eggert, M., & Schwittay, S. (2012a). Generalizability and applicability of model-based business process compliance checking approaches—A state of the art analysis and research roadmap. *Business Research 5*(2), 221–247.

Becker, J., Delfmann, P., & Knackstedt, R. (2007c). Adaptive reference modeling. integrating configurative and generic adaption techniques for information models. In J. Becker & P. Delfmann (Eds.), *Reference modeling. Efficient information systems design through reuse of information models* (pp. 23–49). Berlin: Physica.

Becker, J., Eggert, M., Fleischer, S., Heddier, M., & Knackstedt, R. (2012b). Data warehouse design and legal visualization—The applicability of H_2 for reporting. *23rd Australasian Conference on Information Systems (ACIS)*, Geelong, Australia.

Becker, J., Eggert, M., Heddier, M., & Knackstedt, R. (2012c). Merging conceptual modeling and law for legally compliant information systems design—A framework-based research agenda. *45th Hawaii International Conference on System Sciences (HICSS-45)*, Maui, HI, USA.

Becker, J., Eggert, M., Knackstedt, R., & Fleischer, S. (2012). Fachkonzeptionelle Modellierung Von Berichtspflichten in Finanzaufsicht Und Verwaltung Mit Dem H2-Toolset. *Lecture Notes in Informatics, 197*, 83–96.

Becker, J., Eggert, M., Knackstedt, R., & Winkelmann, A. (2011b). Towards a contingency theory based model of the influence of regulation on Mis. *Americas Conference on Information Systems (AMCIS)*, Detroit, USA.

Becker, J., Eggert, M., & Schwittay, S. (2012e). How to evaluate the practical relevance of business process compliance checking approaches? *Multikonferenz Wirtschaftsinformatik (MKWI)*, Braunschweig, Germany.

Becker, J., Fleischer, S., Janiesch, C., Knackstedt, R., Müller-Wienbergen, F., & Seidel, S. (2007). H2 for REPORTING: Analyse, Konzeption Und Kontinuierliches Metadatenmanagement Von Management-Informations systemen. In J. Becker, H. L. Grob, B. Hellingrath, S. Klein, H. Kuchen, & U. Müller-Funk et al. (Eds.), *Arbeitsberichte des Instituts für Wirtschaftsinformatik*. Muenster: University of Muenster.

Becker, J., Heddier, M., & Knackstedt, R. (2012f). Towards business process modeling in business contracting—Analyzing collaboration contracts as a field of application for process models. *45th Hawaii International Conference on System Sciences (HICSS-45)*, Maui, HI, USA.

Becker, J., & Kahn, D. (2003). The process in focus. In J. Becker, M. Kugler & M. Rosemann (Eds.), *Process management: A guide for the design of business processes*. Berlin: Springer.

Becker, J., & Knackstedt, R. (2003). Konstruktion Und Anwendung Fachkonzeptioneller Referenzmodelle Im Data Warehousing. In W. Esswein, W. Uhr & E. Schopp (Ed.), *Wirtschaftsinformatik 2003. Band Ii. Medien, Märkte, Mobilität* (pp. 415–434). Heidelberg: Physica.

Becker, J., & Knackstedt, R. (2004). Referenzmodellierung Im Data-Warehousing. State-of-the-Art Und Konfigurative Ansätze Für Die Fachkonzeption. *Wirtschaftsinformatik 46*(1), 39–49.

Becker, J., Thome, I., Weiß, B., & Winkelmann, A. (2010). Constructing a semantic business process modelling language for the banking sector—An evolutionary dyadic design science approach. *Enterprise Modelling and Information Systems Architectures, 5*(1), 4–25.

Becker, J., Weiß, B., & Winkelmann, A. (2009). Developing a business process modeling language for the banking sector—A design science approach. *15th Americas Conference on Information Systems (AMCIS)*, San Francisco, CA.

Bellatreche, L., & Mohania, M. (2009). Physical data warehousing design. In J. Wang (Ed.), *Encyclopedia of data warehousing and mining* (pp. 1546–1551). Hershey, PA: IGI Global.

Benbasat, I., Goldstein, D. K., & Mead, M. (1987). The case research strategy in studies of information systems. *MIS Quarterly, 11*(3), 369–386.

Berger-Walliser, G., Bird, R. C., & Haapio, H. (2011). Promoting business success through contract visualization. *Journal of Law, Business, and Ethics 17*(1), 55–75.

Bergeron, B. (2004). *Essentials of XBRL: Financial reporting in the 21st century*. New York: Wiley.

Boehme-Neßler, V. (2005). Visualisierung Des Rechts—Chancen Und Risiken. Rechtstheoretische Anmerkungen Zum Einfluss Der Bilder Auf Das Recht. In E. Hilgendorf (Ed.), *Beiträge Zur Rechtsvisualisierung*. Berlin: Logos Verlag.

Bongaerts, D., & Charlier, E. (2009). Private equity and regulatory capital. *Journal of Banking & Finance, 33*, 1211–1220.

Bonsón, E., Cortijo, V., Escobar, T., Flores, F., & Monreal, S. (2010). Solvency II and XBRL: New rules and technologies in insurance supervision. *Journal of Financial Regulation and Compliance, 18*(2), 144–157.

Boudreau, M.-C., Gefen, D., & Straub, D. W. (2001). Validation in information systems research: A state-of-the-art assessment. *Management Information Systems Quarterly, 25*(1), 1–16.

Breaux, T. D., & Antón, A. I. (2008). Analyzing regulatory rules for privacy and security requirements. *IEEE Transactions on Software Engineering, 34*(1), 5–20.

Breaux, T. D., Antón, A. I., & Spafford, E. H. (2009). A distributed requirements management framework for legal compliance and accountability. *Computers & Security, 28*, 8–17.

Breaux, T. D., Vail, M. W., & Antón, A. I. (2006). Towards regulatory compliance: Extracting rights and obligations to align requirements with regulations. *14th IEEE International Requirements Engineering Conference*, Minneapolis/St. Paul, MN, USA.

Brewer, D. F. C., & Nash, M. J. (1989). *The Chinese wall security policy* (pp. 206–214). *IEEE Symposium on Research in Security and Privacy*, Oakland, CA.

Brinkkemper, S. (1996). Method engineering: Engineering of information systems development methods and tools. *Information and Software Technology, 38*, 275–280.

Brinkkemper, S., Saeki, M., & Harmsen, F. (1999). Meta-modelling based assembly techniques for situational method engineering. *Information Systems, 24*(3), 209–228.

Brunnermeier, M., Crockett, A., Goodhart, C., Persaud, A. D., & Shin, H. (2009). The fundamental principles of financial regulation. *Geneva Reports on the World Economy 11*, Geneva, Switzerland: ICMB International Center for Monetary and Banking Studies.

Brunschwig, C. R. (2006). Visualising legal information: Mind maps and e-Government. *Electronic Government, an International Journal, 3*(4), 386–403.

Brunschwig, C. R. (2012). Multisensory law and therapeutic jurisprudence: How family mediators can better communicate with their clients. *Phoenix Law Review, 5*(4), 705–746.

Bulos, D. (1996). A new dimension. Olap database design. *Database Programming & Design, 9*(6), 33–37.

Bundesbank, D. (2012). Banking supervision form centre. Retrieved July 26, 2012, from http://www.bundesbank.de/Navigation/EN/Service/Reporting_systems/Banking_supervision_form_centre/banking_supervision_form_centre.html.

Carnaghan, C. (2006). Business process modeling approaches in the context of process level audit risk assessment: An analysis and comparison. *International Journal of Accounting Information Systems, 7*(2), 170–204.

Chai, S., Kim, M., & Rao, H. R. (2011). Firms' information security investment decisions: Stock market evidence of investors' behavior. *Decision Support Systems, 50*, 651–661.

Chaudhuri, S., & Umeshwar, D. (1997). An overview of data warehousing and Olap technology. *Newsletter ACM SIGMOD Record, 26*(1), 65–74.

Chen, W., & Hirschheim, R. (2004). A paradigmatic and methodological examination of information systems research from 1991 to 2001. *Information Systems Journal, 14*, 197–235.

Chesani, F., Mello, P., Montali, M., & Storari, S. (2007). Testing careflow process execution conformance by translating a graphical language to computational logic. In R. Bellazzi, A. Abu-Hanna & Hunter, J. (Eds.), *11th Conference on Artificial Intelligence in Medicine, AIME 2007* (pp. 479–488). Amsterdam, The Netherlands: Springer.

Cimatti, A., Clarke, E., Giunchiglia, E., Giunchiglia, F., Pistore, M., & Roveri, M. (2002). Nusmv 2: An opensource tool for symbolic model checking. In E. Brinksma & K. G. Larsen (Eds.), *14th International Conference on Computer Aided Verification (CAV 2002)* (pp. 359–364). Berlin: Springer.

Clark, H. H., & Brennan, S. E. (1996). Grounding in communication. In L. B. Resnick, J. M. Levine & S. D. Teasley (Eds.), *Perspectives on socially shared cognition.* American Psychological Association.

Clarke, E. M. J., Grumberg, O., & Peled, D. A. (2000). *Model checking.* Cambridge, MA, USA: MIT Press.

Colliat, G. (1996). Olap, relational, and multidimensional database systems. *ACM SIGMOD Record, 25*(3), 64–69.

Cowan, K., & de Gregorio, J. (2003). Credit information and market performance: The case of Chile. In M. Miller (Ed.), *Credit reporting systems and the international economy.* Boston: MIT Press.

Craig, R. J., & Diga, J. G. (1996). Financial reporting regulation in ASEAN: Features and prospects. *The International Journal of Accounting, 31*(2), 239–259.

Crook, R., Ince, D., & Nuseibeh, B. (2003). Modelling access policies using roles in requirements engineering. *Information and Software Technology, 45*, 979–991.

Crotty, J. (2009). Structural causes of the global financial crisis: A critical assessment of the 'new financial architecture'. *Cambridge Journal of Economics, 33*(4), 563–580.

Davenport, T. H., & Beers, M. C. (1995). Managing information about processes. *Journal of Management Information Systems, 12*(1), 57–80.

Davenport, T. H., & Stoddard, D. B. (1994). Reengineering: Business change of mythic proportions? *MIS Quarterly, 18*(2), 121–127.

Davis, F. D., Bagozzi, R. P., & Warshaw, P. R. (1989). User acceptance of computer technology: A comparison of two theoretical models. *Management Science, 35*(8), 982–1003.

Debreceny, R. (2007). Research into XBRL—Old and new challenges. In R. Debreceny, C. Felden, & M. Piechocki (Eds.), *New dimensions of business reporting and XBRL* (pp. 3–15). Wiesbaden: Deutscher Universitäts-Verlag.

Debreceny, R., Farewell, S., Piechocki, M., Felden, C., & Gräning, A. (2010). Does It add up? Early evidence on the data quality of XBRL filings to the SEC. *Journal of Accounting and Public Policy, 29*, 296–306.

Debreceny, R., & Gray, G. L. (2001). The production and use of semantically rich accounting reports on the internet: XML and XBRL. *International Journal of Accounting Information Systems, 2*(1), 47–74.

Delfmann, P., Herwig, S., Karow, M., & Lis, L. (2008). Ein Konfiguratives Meta-modellierungswerkzeug. *Modellierung betrieblicher Informationssysteme (MobIS)* (pp. 109–127), Saarbrücken.

Delfmann, P., Herwig, S., & Lis, L. (2009). Unified enterprise knowledge representation with conceptual models—Capturing corporate language in naming conventions. *30th International Conference on Information Systems (ICIS 2009)*, Phoenix, AZ, USA.

Dillmann, D. A., Snyth, J. D., & Christian, L. M. (2009). *Internet, mail, and mixed-mode survey: The tailored design method* (3rd edn.). Hoboken, NJ, US: John Wiley & Sons Inc.

Donaldson, L. (2001). *The contingency theory of organizations*. Thousand Oaks, CA: Sage Publications.

Eggert, M., Knackstedt, R., Fleischer, S., & Becker, J. (2013a). The potential of configurative reference modeling for business to government reporting—A modeling technique and its evaluation. *e-Service Journal* (In Press).

Eggert, M., Winkelmann, A., Lohmann, P., & Knackstedt, R. (2013b). The regulatory influence on management information systems—A contingency perspective. *European Conference on Information Systems (ECIS)*, Utrecht, Netherlands.

El Kharbili, M., De Medeiros, A. K. A., Stein, S., & van der Aalst, W. M. P. (2008). Business process compliance checking: Current state and future challenges. *MoBIS, 2008*, 107–113.

El Kharbili, M., Stein, S., Markovic, I., & Pulvermüller, E. (2008b). Towards a framework for semantic business process compliance management. *Workshop on Governance, Risk and Compliance (GRCIS) at CAiSE*, Montpellier, France.

Elgammal, A., Turetken, O., van den Heuvel, W.-J., & Papazoglou, M. (2010). Root-cause analysis of design-time compliance violations on the basis of property patterns. In P. Maglio, M. Weske, J. Yang & M. Fantinato (Eds.), *Service-oriented computing* (pp. 17–31). Berlin: Springer.

Ernst & Young. (2005). *Global information security survey 2005: Report on the Widening Gap*.

Eshuis, R., & Wieringa, R. (2004). Tool support for verifying UML activity diagrams. *IEEE Transactions on Software Engineering, 30*(7), 437–447.

Fernández-Medina, E., Trujillo, J., Villarroel, R., & Piattini, M. (2006). Access control and audit model for the multidimensional modeling of data warehouses. *Decision Support Systems, 42*, 1270–1289.

Fettke, P. (2006). State-of-the-Art Des State-of-the-Art: Eine Untersuchung Der Forschungs-methode "Review" Innerhalb Der Wirtschaftsinformatik. *Wirtschaftsinformatik, 48*(4), 257–266.

Fettke, P., & Loos, P. (2007a). Perspectives on reference modeling. In P. Fettke, & P. Loos (Eds.), *Reference modeling for business systems analysis* (pp. 1–20). Hershey, PA, USA: IGI Publishing.

Fettke, P., & Loos, P. (2007). *Reference modeling for business analysis*. Hershey, London: Idea Group Publishing.

Fleischer, S. (2013). Konstruktion Und Anwendung Eines Multizweckorientierten Hierarchischen Metamodellierungswerkzeugs. In J. Becker, H. L. Grob, S. Klein, H. Kuchen, U. Müller-Funk, & G. Vossen (Eds.), *Advances in information systems and management science*. Berlin: Logos.

Foerster, A., Engels, G., Schattkowsky, T., & Van Der Straeten, R. (2007). Verification of business process quality constraints based on visual process patterns. *First Joint IEEE/IFIP Symposium on Theoretical Aspects of Software Engineering (TASE '07)*: IEEE (pp. 197–208).

Fontana, A., & Frey, J. H. (2005). The interview: From neural stance to political involvement. In N. K. Denzin & Y. S. Lincoln (Eds.), *The sage handbook of qualitative research*. Thousand Oaks, CA, US: Sage Publications Inc.

Gabriel, R., & Gluchowski, P. (1998). Graphical notation for the semantic modelling of multidimensional data structures in management support systems. *Business & Information Systems Engineering 40*(6), 493–502.

Galbraith, J. R. (1973). *Designinig complex organizations*. Boston, MA, USA: Addison-Wesley.

Ghose, A., & Koliadis, G. (2007). Auditing business process compliance. In B. J. Krämer, K.-J. Lin & P. Narasimhan (Eds.), *Service-oriented computing (ICSOC 2007)* (pp. 169–180). Vienna, Austria: Springer.

Gibson, M., & Arnott, D. (2007). The use of focus groups in design science research. *Australian Conference on Information Systems (ACIS 2007)*.

Goedertier, S., & Vanthienen, J. (2006). Designing compliant business processes with obligations and permissions. In J. Eder & S. Dustdar (Eds.), *Business Process Management Workshops* (pp. 5–14). LNCS vol. 4103. Berlin: Springer.

Goeken, M. (2004). Referenzmodellbasierte Einführung Von Führungsinformationssystemen. Grundlagen, Anforderungen, Methode. *Wirtschaftsinformatik 46*(5), 353–365.

Goeken, M., & Knackstedt, R. (2007). Multidimensional reference models for data warehouse development. In J. Filipe (Ed.), *9th International Conference on Enterprise Information Systems*, Funchal/Portugal.

Goeken, M., & Knackstedt, R. (2008). Referenzmodellgestütztes Compliance Reporting Am Beispiel Der Eu-Finanzmarktrichtlinie Mifid. *HMD—Praxis der Wirtschaftsinformatik, 263*, 47–57.

Goeken, M., & Knackstedt, R. (2009). Multidimensionale Referenzmodelle Zur Unterstützung Des Compliancemanagements Grundlagen - Sprache – Anwendung. In R. Hansen, D. Karagiannis & H.-G. Fill (Eds.), *9. Internationale Tagung Wirtschaftsinformatik* (pp. 359–368) Wien, Austria.

Golfarelli, M., Maio, D., & Rizzi, S. (1998). The dimensional fact model—A conceptual model for data warehouse. *International Journal of Cooperative Information Systems, 7*(2–3), 215–246.

Goodhart, C. A. E. (2008). The regulatory response to the financial crisis. *Journal of Financial Stability, 4*(4), 351–358.

Goossenaerts, J. B. M., Zegers, A. T. M., & Smits, J. M. (2009). A multi-level model-driven regime for value-added tax compliance in ERP systems. *Computers in Industry, 60*, 709–727.

Gordijn, J., & Akkermans, J. M. (2003). Value-based requirements engineering: Exploring innovative e-Commerce ideas. *Requirements Engineering, 8*(2), 114–134.

Governatori, G., Hoffmann, J., Sadiq, S., & Weber, I. (2008). Detecting regulatory compliance for business process models through semantic annotations. *Workshop on Business Process Design*, Milan.

Governatori, G., & Milosevic, Z. (2006). A formal analysis of a business contract language. *International Journal of Cooperative Information Systems, 15*(4), 659–685.

Governatori, G., Milosevic, Z., & Sadiq, S. (2006). Compliance checking between business processes and business contracts. *10th IEEE International Enterprise Distributed Object Computer Conference* (pp. 221–232).

Governatori, G., & Rotolo, A. (2010). A conceptually rich model of business process compliance. In S. Link & A. K. Ghose (Eds.), *Seventh Asia-Pacific Conference on Conceptual Modelling (APCCM '10)* (pp. 3–12). Darlinghurst, Australia: Australian Computer Society.

Hammer, M., & Champy, J. (1993). *Reengineering the corporation: A manifesto for business revolution*. New York: HarperBusiness.

Harmsen, F., Brinkkemper, S., & Oei, H. (1994). Situational method engineering for information system project approaches. In A. A. Verrijn Stuart & T. W. Olle (Eds.), *IFIP WG 8.1 Working Conference*, Maastricht, Netherlands.

Harren, A., & Herden, O. (1999). Mml and Muml—Language and tool for supporting conceptual data warehouse designs. *2.GI-Workshop Data Mining und Data Warehousing (DMDW99)* (pp. 57–68), Magdeburg, Germany.

He, Q., & Antón, A. I. (2009). Requirements-based access control analysis and policy specification (Recaps). *Information and Software Technology, 51*, 993–1009.

Henderson-Sellers, B., & Ralyté, J. (2010). Situational method engineering: State-of-the-art review. *Journal of Universal Computer Science, 16*(3), 424–478.

Henderson, J. C., & Venkatraman, N. (1992). Strategic alignment: A model for organizational transformation through information technology. In T. A. Kocham & M. Useem (Eds.), *Transforming organizations*. New York: Oxford University Press.

Hettler, D., Preuss, P., & Niedereichholz, J. (2003). Vergleich Ausgewählter Ansätze Zur Semantischen Modellierung Von Data-Warehouse-Systemen. *HMD—Praxis der Wirtschaftsinformatik, 231*, 97–107.

Hevner, A. R., March, S. T., Park, J., & Ram, S. (2004). Design science in information systems research. *Mis Quarterly, 28*(1), 75–105.

Holten, R. (2003). Specification of management views in information warehouse projects. *Information Systems, 28*(7), 709–751.

Hüsemann, B., Lechtenbörger, J., & Vossen, G. (2000). Conceptual Datawarehouse design. *International Workshop on Design and Management of DataWarehouses (DMDW'2000)*, Stockholm, Sweden.

Iivari, J., Hirschheim, R., & Klein, H. K. (1998). A paradigmatic analysis contrasting information systems development approaches and methodologies. *Information Systems Research, 9*(2), 164–193.

Ingolfo, S., Siena, A., Mylopoulos, J., Susi, A., & Perini, A. (2013). Arguing regulatory compliance of software requirements. *Data & Knowledge Engineering* (In press).

Inmon, W. H. (1996). *Building the data warehouse* (2nd ed.). New York: Wiley.

Julisch, K., Suter, C., Woitalla, T., & Zimmermann, O. (2011). Compliance by design—Bridging the chasm between auditors and it architects. *Computers & Security, 30*, 410–426.

Kabilan, V. (2005). Contract workflow model patterns using BPMN. *10th International Workshop on Exploring Modeling Methods in Systems Analysis and Design (EMMSAD 05)* (pp. 557–568), Porto, Portugal.

Karagiannis, D. (2008). A business process-based modelling extension for regulatory compliance. *Multikonferenz Wirtschaftsinformatik (MKWI 2008)* (pp. 1159–1173). Munich, Germany.

Kardasis, P., & Loucopoulos, P. (2004). Expressing and organising business rules. *Information and Software Technology, 46*, 701–718.

Karlsson, L., Dahlstedt, A. G., & och Dag, J. N. (2002). Challenges in market-driven requirements engineering—An industrial interview study. *Proceedings of Eighth International Workshop on Requirements Engineering: Foundation for Software Quality*, Essen, Germany.

Kartseva, V., Gordijn, J., & Tan, Y.-H. (2005). Toward a modeling tool for designing control mechanisms for network organizations. *International Journal of Electronic Commerce, 10*(2), 57–84.

Keller, G., Nüttgens, M., & Scheer, A.-W. (1992). Semantische Prozeßmodellierung Auf Der Grundlage Ereignisgesteuerter Prozeßketten (Epk). In A.-W. Scheer (Ed.), *Veröffentlichungen Des Instituts Für Wirtschaftsinformatik*, Saarbrücken.

Kernan, K. (2008). XBRL around the world. *Journal of Accountancy, 206*(4), 62–66.

Kerrigan, S., & Law, K. H. (2003). Logic-based regulation compliance-assistance. *9th International Conference on AI and Law (ICAIL)* (pp. 126–135), Edinburgh, Scotland, UK.

Knackstedt, R., Brelage, C., & Kaufmann, N. C. (2006). Development of web-applications in consideration of legal requirements—Juridical framework, state-of-the-art and conceptual modelling. *Wirtschaftsinformatik, 48*(1), 27–35.

Knackstedt, R., Eggert, M., & Fleischer, S. (2012). The legal perspective on business to government reporting—A conceptual modeling approach and its application in the financial sector. *45th Hawaii International Conference on System Sciences*, Maui, HI, USA.

Knackstedt, R., Eggert, M., Gräwe, L., & Spittka, J. (2010). Forschungsportal Für Rechtsinformatik Und Informationsrecht. *Multimedia und Recht (MMR), 8*, 528–533.

Knackstedt, R., Eggert, M., Heddier, M., Chasin, F., & Becker, J. (2013). The relationship of IS and law—The perspective of and implications for IS research. *European Conference on Information Systems (ECIS)*, Utrecht, Netherlands.

Knackstedt, R., & Klose, K. (2005). Configurative reference model-based development of data warehouse systems. *16th Information Resources Management Association Conference (IRMA)* (pp. 32–39), San Diego, USA.

Knackstedt, R., Klose, K., Niehaves, B., & Becker, J. (2005). Process reference model for data warehouse development—A Consensus oriented approach. In C.-S. Chen (Ed.), *ICEIS 2005, Proceedings of the Seventh International Conference on Enterprise Information Systems* (pp. 499–505), Miami, USA.

Kuester, J. M., Ryndina, K., & Gall, H. (2007). Generation of business process models for object life cycle compliance. In G. Alonso, P. Dadam, & M. Rosemann (Eds.), *Business process management* (pp. 165–181). Springer: Berlin.

Kung, C.H., & Sölvberg, A. (1986). Activity modelling and behaviour modelling. In T. W. Olle, H. G. Sol & A. A. Verrijn-Stuart (Eds.), *Information systems design methodologies: Improving the practice, IFIP* (pp. 145–171). Amsterdam, North-Holland.

Kvale, S. (1996). *Interviews: An introduction to qualitative research interviewing*. Thousand Oaks, CA, USA: Sage Publications.

Lang, K., & Bodendorf, F. (1997). Gestaltung Von Geschäftsprozessen Auf Der Basis Von Prozessbausteinbibliotheken. In H. Heilmann & S. Meinhardt (Eds.), *Business process (Re-) engineering*, (pp. 83–94). Berlin: dpunkt

Lawrence, P. R., & Lorsch, J. W. (1967). Differentiation and integration in complex organizations. *Administrative Science Quarterly, 12*, 1–47.

Liu, K., Sun, L., Dix, A., & Narasipuram, M. (2001). Norm-based agency for designing collaborative information systems. *Information Systems Journal, 11*, 229–247.

Liu, Y., Müller, S., & Xu, K. (2007). A static compliance-checking framework for business process models. *IBM Systems Journal, 46*(2), 335–361.

Lu, R., Sadiq, S., & Governatori, G. (2008). Compliance aware business process design. In A. ter Hofstede, B. Benatallah, & H.-Y. Paik (Eds.), *Business process management workshops* (pp. 120–131). Berlin: Springer.

Lu, R., Sadiq, S., & Governatori, G. (2008). Measurement of compliance distance in business processes. *Information Systems Management, 25*(4), 344–355.

Ly, L., Rinderle-Ma, S., Göser, K., & Dadam, P. (2012). On enabling integrated process compliance with semantic constraints in process management systems requirements, challenges, solutions. *Information Systems Frontier, 19*(2), 195–219.

Ly, L. T., Goeser, K., Rinderle-Ma, S., & Dadam, P. (2008). Compliance of semantic constraints—A requirements analysis for process management systems. In S. Sadiq, M. Indulska, M. zur Muehlen, X. Franch, E. Hunt & R. Coletta (Eds.), *Proceedings of the International Workshop on Governance, Risk and Compliance-Applications in Information Systems* (pp. 31–45), Montpellier, France.

Ly, L.T., Rinderle-Ma, S., & Dadam, P. (2006). Semantic correctness in adaptive process management systems. In S. Dustdar, J. L. Fiadeiro & A. Sheth (Eds.), *Business process management 4th International Conference (BPM 2006)* (pp. 193–208). Vienna Austria: Springer

Mahler, T. (2010). *Legal risk management: developing and evaluation elements of a method for proactive legal analyses, with a particular focus on contracts*. PhD Thesis, Faculty of Law, University of Oslo.

March, S. T., & Smith, G. F. (1995). Design and natural science research on information technology. *Decision Support Systems, 15*(4), 251–266.

Massacci, F., Mylopoulos, J., & Zannone, N. (2007). From hippocratic databases to secure tropos: A computer-aided re-engineering approach. *International Journal of Software Engineering, 17*(2), 265–284.

Massacci, F., Prest, M., & Zannone, N. (2005). Using a security requirements engineering methodology in practice: The compliance with the italian data protection legislation. *Computer Standard Interfaces, 27*(5), 445–455.

Massey, A. K., Otto, P. N., Heyward, L. J., & Antón, A. I. (2012). Evaluating existing security and privacy requirements for legal compliance. *Requirements Engineering, 15*, 119–137.

McCloskey, M. J. (1998). Visualizing the law: Methods for mapping the legal landscape and drawing analogies. *Washington Law Review, 73*(1), 163–192.

McCutcheon, D. M., & Meredith, J. R. (1993). Conducting case study research in operations management. *Journal of Operations Management, 11*(3), 239–256.

McGreevy, M. (2008). Amr research finds spending on governance, risk management, and compliance will exceed \$32b in 2008. Boston: AMR Research, Inc.

Milner, R. (1999). *Communicating and mobile systems: The Π-calculus.* Cambridge, UK: Cambridge University Press.

Milosevic, Z. (2005). Towards Integrating Business Policies with Business Processes. In W. M. P. van der Aalst, B. Benatallah, F. Casati & F. Curbera (Eds.), *3rd International Conference on Business Process Management (BPM 2005) Nancy,* (pp. 404–409), France.

Milosevic, Z., Josang, A., Dimitrakos, T., & Patton, M. (2002). Discretionary enforcement of electronic contracts. In *Sixth International Conference on Enterprise Distributed Object Computing Conference (EDOC '02)* Los Alamitos: IEEE Computer Society, pp. 3–14.

Mingers, J. (2001). Combining is research methods: towards a pluralist methodology. *Information Systems Research, 12*(3), 240–259.

Mouratidisa, H., Islama, S., Kalloniatisb, C., & Gritzalis, S. (2013). A framework to support selection of cloud providers based on security and privacy requirements. *The Journal of Systems and Software* (In press).

Mueller, J. (2010). *Strukturbasierte verifikation von Bpmn-modellen.* Tübingen: University of Tübingen.

Mylopoulos, J. (1992). Conceptual modelling and telos. In P. Loucopoulos & R. Zicari (Eds.), *Conceptual modelling, databases, and case: An integrated view of information system development* (pp. 49–68). New York: Wiley.

Mylopoulos, J. (1998). Information modeling in the time of the revolution. *Information Systems, 23*(3/4), 127–155.

Oates, B. J. (2006). *Researching information systems and computing.* London, UK: Sage Publications Inc.

Object Management Group. (2005). *Unified modelling language: Superstructure,* (Version 2.0, formal/4.7.2005 Edn.). Needham: Object Management Group.

Object Management Group. (2006). *Business process modelling notation specification: Final adopted specification,* (dtc/1.2 Edn.). Needham: Object Management Group.

Olbrich, S., & Simon, C. (2008). Process modelling towards e-government: Visualisation and semantic modelling of legal regulations as executable process sets. *The Electronic Journal of e-Government, 6*(1), 43–54.

Oppitz, U.-D. (1990). *Deutsche Rechtsbücher Des Mittelalters: Beschreibung Der Handschriften.* Böhlau.

Orlikowski, W., & Baroudi, J. J. (1991). Studying information technology in organizations: Research approaches and assumptions. *Information Systems Research, 2*, 1–28.

Otto, P.N., & Antón, A. (2007). *Addressing legal requirements in requirements engineering. 15th IEEE International Requirements Engineering Conference,* India Habitat Centre, New Delhi.

Parker, M. M., Benson, R. J., & Trainor, H. E. (1988). *Information economics: Linking business performance to information technology.* Englewood Cliffs: Prentice Hall.

Peffers, K., Tuunanen, T., Rothenberger, M. A., & Chatterjee, S. (2007). A design science research methodology for information systems research. *Journal of Management Information Systems, 24*(3), 45–77.

Pfeiffer., D. (2008). *Semantic business process analysis: Building block-based construction of automatically analysable business process models, Doctroal Thesis.* University of Muenster.

Pfeiffer, F., & Flöck, D. (2011). Orinoco—Eine Bpm-/Soa-Erfolgsgeschichte in Der Deutschen Bank. In A. Komus (Ed.), *Bpm best practice*. Berlin: Springer.

Pinsonneault, A., & Kraemer, K. L. (1993). Survey research methodology in management information systems: An assessment. *Journal of Management Information Systems, 10*(2), 75–105.

Podsakoff, P. M., MacKenzie, S. B., Lee, J.-Y., & Podsakoff, N. P. (2003). Common method biases in behavioral research: A critical review of the literature and recommended remedies. *Journal of Applied Psychology, 88*(5), 879–903.

Priebe, T., & Pernul, G. (2001). *Metadaten-Gestützer Data-Warehouse-Entwurf Mit Adapted1 Uml. 5th Internationale Tagung Wirtschaftsinformatik (WI 2001)*, Augsburg, Germany.

Raduescu, C., Tan, H. M., Jayaganesh, M., Bandara, W., zur Muehlen, M., & Lippe, S. (2006). *A framework of issues in large process modeling projects. Proceedings of the European Conference on Information Systems (ECIS 2006)* (pp. 1–12), Göteborg, Sweden.

Ralyté, J., Rolland, C., & Deneckère, R. (2004). Towards a meta-tool for change-centric method engineering: A typology of generic operators. In A. Persson & J. Stirna (Eds.), *Advanced Information Systems Engineering 16th International Conference (CAiSE 2004)*, Riga, Latvia.

Ramezani, E., Fahland, D., & van der Aalst, W. M. P. (2012). Diagnostic information in compliance checking. *BPM Center Report BPM-12-11* Retrieved July 09, 2012, from http://bpmcenter.org/wp-content/uploads/reports/2012/BPM-12-11.pdf.

Raus, M., Flügge, B., & Bouttellier, R. (2009). Electronic customs innovation: an improvement of governmental infrastructures. *Government Information Quarterly, 26*, 246–256.

Recker, J., Rosemann, M., Indulska, M., & Green, P. (2009). Business process modeling: A comparative analysis. *Journal of the Association for Information Systems, 10*(4), 333–363.

Ringle, C. M., Wende, S., & Will, A. (2005). *Smartpls—Version 2.0.M3*. Hamburg: University of Hamburg.

Risto, H. (2001). Deontic Logic. In L. Goble (Ed.), *The Blackwell guide to philosophical logic*. Oxford: Blackwell Publishers.

Rizzi, S., Abelló, A., Lechtenbörger, J., & Trujillo, J. (2006). *Research in data warehouse modeling and design: Dead or alive?. 9th ACM international workshop on Data warehousing and OLAP (DOLAP '06)*, (pp. 3–10). Arlington, Virginia, USA.

Rosca, D., & Wild, C. (2002). Towards a flexible deployment of business rules. *Expert Systems with Applications, 23*, 385–394.

Rosemann, M. (2003). Preparation of process modeling. In J. Becker, M. Kugler, & M. Rosemann (Eds.), *Process management: A guide for the design of business processes*. Berlin: Springer.

Rosemann, M., & de Bruin, T. (2005). Towards a business process management maturity model. In *Proceedings of the 13th European Conference on Information Systems*. Regensburg, Germany.

Rosemann, M., & Vessey, I. (2008). Toward improving the relevance of information systems research to practice: The role of applicability checks. *Management Information Systems Quarterly, 32*, 1–22.

Rossak, W., Foetsch, D., & Pulvermueller, E. (2006). *Modeling and verifying workflow-based regulations. International workshop on regulations modeling and their validation and verification (REMO2V06)*, pp. 825–830. Luxemburg.

Rowley, J., & Slack, F. (2004). Conducting a literature review. *Management Research News, 27*(6), 31–39.

Rozinat, A., & van der Aalst, W. M. P. (2008). Conformance checking of processes based on monitoring real behavior. *Information Systems, 33*(1), 64–95.

Sachs-Hombach, K. (2005). Vom Text Zum Bild—Wege Für Das Recht. In E. Hilgendorf (Ed.), *Beiträge Zur Rechtsvisualisierung*. Berlin: Logos Verlag.

Sadiq, S., Governatori, G., & Namiri, K. (2007). Modeling control objectives for business process compliance. In G. Alonso, P. Dadam, & M. Rosemann (Eds.), *Business Process Management Journal* (pp. 149–164). Berlin: Springer.

Sapia, C., Blaschka, M., Höfling, G., & Dinter, B. (1998). Extending the E/R model for the multidimensional paradigm. *International Workshop on Data Warehouse and Data Mining (DWDM'98)* (pp. 105–116), Singapur.

Scapens, R. W. (1990). Researching management accounting practice: The role of case study methods. *The British Accounting Review, 22*(3), 259–281.

Schumm, D., Turetken, O., Kokash, N., Elgammal, A., Leymann, F., & van den Heuvel, W.-J. (2010). Business process compliance through reusable units of compliant processes. In F. Daniel & F. M. Facca (Eds.), *Current trends in web engineering* (pp. 325–237). Berlin: Springer.

Stewart, D. W., Shamdasani, P. N., and Rook, D. W. (2007). *Focus groups: Theory and practice*, (2 ed.). California: Sage Publications.

Tanur, J. M. (1982). Advances in methods for large-scale surveys and experiments: A National resource, Part 11. In R. Mcadams, N. J. Smelser, & D. J. Treiman (Eds.), *Behavioral and social science*. Washington, DC: National Academy Press.

Thomas, O. (2007). Version management for reference models: Design and implementation. In J. Becker & P. Delfmann (Eds.), *Reference modeling*. Heidelber: Physica-Verlag.

Thomas, O., & Fellmann, M. (2009). Semantic process modeling: Design and implementation of an ontology-based representation of business processes. *Business & Information Systems Engineering, 1*(6), 438–451.

Toval, A., Olmos, A., & Piattini, M. (2002) *Legal requirements reuse: A critical success factor for requirements quality and personal data protection. IEEE Joint International Conference on Requirements Engineering (RE'02)*. Essen, Germany.

Tremblay, M. C., Hevner, A. R., & Berndt, D. J. (2010). The use of focus groups in design science research. *Design research in information systems* (pp. 121–143). Boston, MA: Springer.

Tryfona, N., Busborg, F., & Christianson, J.G.B. (1999). *Starer—a conceptual model for data warehouse design. ACM Second International Workshop on Data Warehousing and OLAP (DOLAP'99)*, Kansas City, USA.

Tsai, H., Chang, Y., & Hsiao, P.-H. (2011). What drives foreign expansion of the top 100 multinational banks? The role of the credit reporting system. *Journal of Banking & Finance, 35*(3), 588–605.

van der Aalst, W.M.P., de Beer, H.T., & van Dongen, B.F. (2005). Process mining and verification of properties: An approach based on temporal logic. In R. Meersman, Z. Tari, M.-S. Hacid, J. John Mylopoulos, B. Barbara Pernici, Ö. Özalp Babaoglu et al. (Eds.), *Confederated International Conference on the Move to Meaningful Internet Systems (OTM '05)*, Agia Napa, Cyprus: Springer, pp. 130–147.

Vassiliadis, P., & Sellis, T. (1999). A survey of logical models for olap databases. *SIGMOD Record, 28*(4), 64–69.

Venkatesh, V., & Bala, H. (2008). Technology acceptance model 3 and a research agenda on interventions. *Decision Sciences, 39*(2), 273–315.

Venkatesh, V., & Davis, F. D. (2000). A theoretical extension of the technology acceptance model: Four longitudinal field studies. *Management Science, 46*(2), 186–204.

Venkatesh, V., Morris, M. G., Davis, G. B., & Davis, F. D. (2003). User acceptance of information technology: Toward a Unified View. pp. 425–478.

Vessey, I., Ramesh, V., & Glass, R. L. (2002). Research in information systems: An empirical study of diversity in the discipline and its journals. *Journal of Management Information Systems, 19*(2), 129–174.

vom Brocke, J. (2002). *Referenzmodellierung. Gestaltung Und Verteilung Von Konstruktions-prozessen*. Muenster, Germany: University of Muenster.

vom Brocke, J., Simons, A., Niehaves, B., Riemer, K., Plattfaut, R., & Cleven, A. (2009). *Reconstructing the giant: On the importance of rigour in documenting the literature search process, Proceedings of the 17th European Conference on Information Systems*, (pp. 2206–2217). Verona, Italy.

von Wright, G.H. (1951). Deontic Logic. *Mind, New Series* (60:237).

Vossen, G. (2008). *Datenmodelle, Datenbanksprachen Und Datenbankmanagementsysteme* (5th ed.). München, Wien: Oldenbourg.

Wan-Kadir, W. M. N., & Loucopoulos, P. (2004). Relating evolving business rules to software design. *Journal of Systems Architecture, 50,* 367–382.

Wand, Y., & Weber, R. (2002). Research commentary: Information systems and conceptual modeling: A research agenda. *Information Systems Research, 13*(4), 363–376.

Weber, M., & Weisbrod, J. (2002). *Requirements engineering in automotive development-experiences and challenges. IEEE Joint International Conference on Requirements Engineering (RE'02)*, Essen, Germany, pp. 331–340

Webster, J., & Watson, R. T. (2002). Analyzing the past to prepare for the future: Writing a literature review. *MIS Quarterly, 26(2),* xiii–xxiii.

Weigand, H., & van den Heuvel, J. (2002). Cross-organizational workflow integration using contracts. *Decision Support Systems, 33*(3), 247–265.

Weigand, H., van den Heuvel, W.-J., & Hiel, M. (2011). Business policy compliance in service-oriented systems. *Information Systems, 36,* 791–807.

Weill, P., & Olson, M. H. (1989). An assessment of the contingency theory of management information systems. *Journal of Management Information Systems, 6*(1), 59–85.

Weiß., B. (2011). Process modelling and analysis in banks: Leveraging business process optimisation in the financail sector, doctoral thesis. Muenster, Germany: University of Muenster.

Weiß, B., & Winkelmann, A. (2011). *A metamodel based perspective on the adaptation of a semantic business process modeling language to the financial sector. 44th Hawaii International Conference on System Sciences*, Hawaii, U.S.

Williams, S. P., Scifleet, P. A., & Hardy, C. A. (2006). Online business reporting: An information management perspective. *International Journal of Information Management, 26*(2), 91–101.

Winter, R. (2008). Design science research in Europe. *European Journal of Information Systems, 17,* 470–475.

Woerzberger, R., Kurpick, T., & Heer, T. (2008a). Checking correctness and compliance of integrated process models. In V. Negru, T. Jebelean, D. Petcu & D. Zaharie (Eds.), *10th International Symposium on Symbolic and Numeric Algorithms for Scientific Computing,* (pp. 576–583), Timisoara, Romania: IEEE Computer Society.

Woerzberger, R., Kurpick, T., & Heer, T. (2008b). *On correctness, compliance and consistency of process models. 17th IEEE International Workshops on Enabling Technologies (WETICE '08)*, (pp. 251–252), Rome, Italy: IEEE Computer Society.

Yagelski, R. P., & Miller, R. K. (2012). *The informed argument* (8th ed.). Belmont, MA, US: Wadsworth.

Yin, R. K. (2003). *Applications of case study research* (2nd ed.). Thousand Oaks: Sage Publications Inc.